CABBAGE

Edible

Series Editor: Andrew F. Smith

EDIBLE is a revolutionary series of books dedicated to food and drink that explores the rich history of cuisine. Each book reveals the global history and culture of one type of food or beverage.

Already published

Cabbage

A Global History

Meg Muckenhoupt

REAKTION BOOKS

*To my husband Scott, who has accompanied me on
so many culinary adventures.*

Published by Reaktion Books Ltd
Unit 32, Waterside
44–48 Wharf Road
London N1 7UX, UK
www.reaktionbooks.co.uk

First published 2018

Printed and bound in China

A catalogue record for this book is available from the British Library

ISBN 978 1 78023 981 1

Contents

I

Cabbage in the Garden of Eden

Diogenes was washing some cabbage leaves when he saw
Aristippus go by. 'If you knew how to live on cabbage,'
Diogenes said, 'you would not be courting a tyrant.'
Aristippus retorted, 'You would not be here washing
cabbages if you knew how to live among men.'
Michel de Montaigne, *The Complete Essays*

Cabbage is confounding. How could a vegetable be so beloved, so universal and so disdained? Cabbage is an essential ingredient in dozens of iconic ethnic dishes – and yet it is almost universally snubbed in restaurants. In recent decades beetroot, rocket salad (or arugula), portobello mushrooms and even cabbage's kissing cousin kale have become international food stars, but cabbage is still a culinary understudy. Banish sauerkraut, and banish all the world: German sauerkraut and *Rotkohl*, Korean kimchi, Polish galumpkis, Russian shchi and borscht soups (also claimed by every other nation from the Baltics to the Black Sea), Norwegian lamb and cabbage *Fårikål*, Irish colcannon, Irish American corned beef and cabbage, the cabbage rolls (*sarmale*) of the Balkans, Middle East, and Eastern and Western Europe, and the *curtido* that accompanies pupusas in Latin American countries.

Cabbage's Many Manifestations

Even simply defining cabbage is confusing. In both Europe and North America, cabbage arrives as a head of *Brassica oleracea*, a bundle of crunchy, compact, vaguely sweet, juicy leaves – but its nearest genetic relatives include kale, broccoli, cauliflower and dry, scruffy, scanty-leaved weeds that chiefly appeal to goats. Cabbage can be either green or red, smooth or savoyed (wrinkled), headed or loose-leaved. Superficially similar-looking plants such as heading cabbage and Chinese or napa cabbage come from different genuses. European cabbages are closely related to kale and cauliflower, while the napa cabbages' nearest genetic relatives are turnips.

One thing is clear: cabbage is a survivor. Its many variations can survive salt, pests, heavy metals and drought, partly because cabbage and its cruciferous relatives are so keen on interbreeding and creating new species. As the mythic Greek Titans spawned the gods of Mount Olympus, so three original groups of crucifers have crossed and re-crossed to create subgroups of crucifers over the millennia, even though they first diverged more than 20 million years ago. Unlike the Titans, the first cabbage clans are still at large. The three original cabbage species are:

> *Brassica oleracea*, or the cabbages. This is the species of the shrubby-leaved weeds that were refined to create modern headed cabbage. Breeders also moulded wayward cabbage plants into kale, Brussels sprouts, broccoli, cauliflower and kohlrabi.

> *Brassica rapa*, or the turnips. This species includes both turnips, which are mainly grown for their roots, and the

many variants of Chinese cabbage, which are valued for their edible leaves.

Brassica nigra, or black mustard. Humans breed these plants for their seeds, which are commonly used as a spice in Indian cooking and have some medicinal applications. These varieties are the ones most inclined towards world domination: *B. nigra* is considered an invasive weed in California, New Zealand, Hawaii and the off-shore islands of Chile, and is either native to or has naturalized in vast swathes of North America, South America, Oceania, Asia and North Africa.

A second set of cabbagey plants arose from spontaneous crosses between the original three. In quasi-mathematical layman's terms:

Cabbage × turnips = *Brassica napus*, the group that includes rapeseed (canola) and swedes.

Cabbage × black mustard = *Brassica carinata*, or Ethiopian mustard. Heat and drought tolerant, this brassica is grown for oilseeds and for its leaves.

Black mustard × turnips = *Brassica juncea*, also known as Chinese mustard or Indian mustard. Subspecies are grown for their seeds, leaves and roots.

The 'Triangle of U', conceived in 1935 by a Korean Japanese botanist variously named Woo Jang-choon or Nagaharu U, illustrates how three different species of brassicas have cross-bred to create food crops.

Curiously, brassica fans in different parts of the world seem to have a knack for breeding similar-looking plants out

Brassica nigra (black mustard).

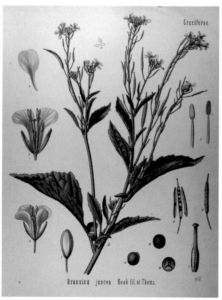

Brassica juncea (Indian or Chinese mustard).

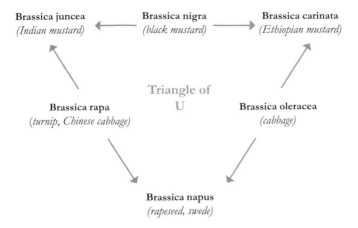

Brassica juncea
(Indian mustard)

Brassica nigra
(black mustard)

Brassica carinata
(Ethiopian mustard)

Triangle of
U

Brassica rapa
(turnip, Chinese cabbage)

Brassica oleracea
(cabbage)

Brassica napus
(rapeseed, swede)

of different genuses. European *Brassica rapa* (rapini) resembles broccoli (*Brassica oleracea* var. *italica*), while Asian *Brassica rapa* (napa cabbage) looks like headed cabbage (*Brassica oleracea* var. *capitata*). Pretty much any *Brassica* plant form you like – heading, with long stems, loose heads, savoyed with wrinkled leaves – can be found in a *Brassica oleracea* from Europe, a *Brassica rapa* from China or Southeast Asia, or a *Brassica juncea* (mustard) from China or Japan. These genetic substitutions probably emerged via breeding to suit local cooking habits rather than with any ecological adaptations by the plants.

All these curious matings and cross-continental peregrinations did not produce the solid head of cabbage we know and loathe (sometimes) today. The greatest variety of wild brassicas grow in the southwest Mediterranean and the Himalayas. At some point, someone decided that the stringy, mustardy leaves of some wild *Brassica* species were worth eating, and started selecting the milder, fleshier plants for cultivation.

Out of Africa:
Cabbage's Continental Origins

Cabbages are a scion of the *Brassica* genus, shape-shifting plants that originated 24 million years ago. They emerged in the Sahara–Sindian belt of land stretching from what is now northwest Africa to India. When tectonic plates shifted 23 million years ago and the Anatolian plate smashed into Africa and Arabia, the Mediterranean sea was cut off from the Indian ocean, and the compressed continents were suddenly joined by a new land bridge. The brassicas seized their opportunity to cross the land bridge and spread rapidly to this newly available environment.

The ancestor of *Brassica oleracea*, our heading cabbage kin, lit out for the eastern Mediterranean, while the progenitors of *Brassica nigra*, the family of black mustards, headed towards central and southern Europe. Protean brassicas diversified in their Grecian lairs, creating the *Brassica oleracea* and *Brassica rapa* lineages. *Brassica oleracea* spread northward to the rest of Europe, while *Brassica rapa* plants arrived in central Asia around 2 million years ago.

And this is part of cabbage's confusion. For most species, animal, vegetable and other, the place where you find most genetic diversity is the place where they first emerged. Brassicas ignored that rule. Cabbages originated in North Africa, where they still grow, but they truly flourished once they reached the eastern Mediterranean. They spawned new forms thousands of miles from their ancestral home, forming new natural hybrids in the Irano-Turanian region in the Near East where Central Asia and the Mediterranean meet. By contrast, the wild 'cole crops' growing on Dover's cliffs and France's fields are genetically homogeneous and closely related to domesticated forms, and appear to be feral escapees rather than prehistorically 'native' plants. Genetic and linguistic evidence points to cabbage first being domesticated in Greece, then spreading to Great Britain – perhaps after the Celts invaded what is now Spain in the sixth to eighth centuries BCE.

Taming the Wild Cabbage

The first domesticated cabbages weren't bred for their leaves. They were grown for seeds. Chinese cabbage is a variety of *Brassica rapa*, and is the beloved base of kimchi and much of Asian cuisine. It was probably first introduced to India and China as a plant that bears oilseeds – seeds of *Brassica rapa* more than 6,000 years old have been found at the Banpo archaeological site outside Xi'an, China, and there is genetic evidence that at least two distinct sub-species of *Brassica rapa* were carried to China and India along standard Silk Road trade routes. By contrast, remnants of charred Brassicaceae family oilseeds of either a wild mustard or radish dated to around 3000 BCE were found in the Temple Oval at the Khafajah site in modern-day Iraq.

There are references to oilseed crops in Indian Aryan literature going back as far as 1500 BCE, and Indians mentioned *Brassica rapa* in the form of yellow sarson, a sort of mustard green, under the name *Siddhartha* in Sanskrit literature in 1000 BCE.

Oilseed-bearing *Brassica rapa* was probably introduced to China in the first century CE. Cabbage seeds were an important crop in China through the seventeenth century, when the *Thien Kung Khai Wu* (The Exploitation of the Works of Nature) stated, 'For eating, the oils of sesame seeds, turnip seeds, yellow soy beans, and cabbage seeds are best.' Cabbage seeds yielded the modern equivalent of 3 litres of oil per 12 litres of seeds, according to the author – the same yield as rapeseed and much less than sesame. Among the brassicas grown for greens, bok choy or pak choy-style greens with thick stems and loose tops seem to have developed first, judging by the number of genetic and leaf variations the wild types display, while loose Chinese cabbage was hybridized from bok choy and turnips in the city of Yangzhou in the tenth century. Chinese breeders had tightened up the heads by the seventeenth century, and the fashionable new cabbage reached Japan by the nineteenth century. Japanese farmers selected a variety that probably cross-bred with local *Brassica juncea* plants to create mizuna and mibuna greens.

The Name of the Cabbage

Linguistic and genetic evidence indicates *Brassica oleracea* cabbages were first domesticated by Greek and Roman gardeners, then spread around Europe by the ancient Roman armies. Cabbages and kales do not appear in other early botanies. They were not listed in the plants found in the Babylonian garden of the monarch Marduk-apla-iddina II, aka Merodach-Baladan, in Babylonia during the late eighth century BCE. A clay cuneiform tablet in the British Museum lists the Akkadian names of 61 plants found in Merodach-Baladan's garden, including lettuce, cucumbers, onions, garlic, beetroot, radishes and turnips – another brassica – but no cabbage.

Cabbages also are not among the many vegetables mentioned in the Bible, the Jewish Mishnah or the Upanishads. Brassicas only show up in the Christian New Testament in the form of *Brassica nigra* ('If you have faith the size of a mustard seed . . .', Mark 13:31). Some archaeologists have claimed that the ancient Egyptians grew cabbage, but there doesn't seem

American-grown 'baby' (immature) bok choy.

to be any mention of cabbage in ancient hieroglyphics or papyri (the closest is a reference to *shaut*, which can also be translated as 'vegetables'). There is no unique ancient Egyptian word for 'cabbage'; the term in various Egyptian dialects is clearly descended from the ancient Greek word for cabbage, *krambe*.

Most words for cabbage around Europe originate with the Romans or the Greeks. The Greeks referred to cabbages with the words *braske*, *kaulos*, *krambe*, *kyma* (for young cabbage shoots), *olyra* and *raphanos*, while Latin included *brassica*, *caulis*, *crambe*, *cyma* and *holus*. 'Brassica' may come from *praesica*, to cut, or *brasso*, to make noise, from the sound the plant makes when broken. Another Greek-derived word the Romans used for cole crops, *caulis*, descends from the Greek word for 'spear-shaft' or 'stem' – a very prominent feature of old leggy kale plants. The cheerful Romans adopted the word and extended it to mean 'penis' as well, before exporting it to dozens of languages around Europe at the pointy ends of Roman spears. German *Kohl*, English kale and Portuguese *couve* all enjoy Roman ancestry, as do Irish *braissech* and Welsh *bresych*. The Latin word for head, *caput*, began to be applied to cabbages in the Middle Ages, giving us the word 'cabbage', Russian *kaputska* and the Old French *caboche* (and, by descent, *choux*). Several Romance languages and German use a word derived from *caulis* (meaning either the cabbage or its stem): German *Kohl*, Irish *cal*; while Celtic *bresich* and *brasic* descend from Roman *brassica*. The fact that all the 'wild' forms of cabbage in Great Britain appear to be genetically homogeneous – suggesting that they are escaped cultivated plants – and that all recorded words for cabbage are derived from Greek strongly implies that the Celts, and Britain, got their beloved cabbage from Greek traders, perhaps as early as 600 BCE, when the Greek Massalia/Marseille colony was established across the channel in France.

Various authors have claimed that the Greeks, Romans or Celts domesticated cabbages in the first century BCE. Leafy kales appear in Greek literature beginning in the sixth century BCE. Greek writers enjoyed separating them into three categories, but exactly what those three categories were changed over time. Theophrastus in the fourth century BCE defined them as curly leaved, smooth leaved and wild, while Eudemus in the third century BCE called them maritime, smooth leaved and celery like. Nicander, in the second century BCE, said that the categories were smooth, curly and purple. Note the absence of the descriptions 'headed', 'only fit for the poor' and 'smelly when boiled'.

While the Greek attitude towards cabbage was take-it-or-leave-it, the Romans fawned over the stuff. Roman Marcus Cato's *De agricultura* (On Agriculture) features a section popularly known as 'In Praise of Cabbage'. He begins by stating, 'Of the medicinal value of the cabbage: it is the cabbage which surpasses all other vegetables,' then goes on to quote dozens of nostrums distilled directly from Greek medical literature. However, Cato uses a word of Greek origin, *brassica*, which appears to have meant any wild kales available to Romans, to name this apex of vegetal achievement. The first recorded mention of cabbages having heads is attributed to Pliny the Elder, who described 87 types in his *Natural History* of 77 CE. Turnips, by contrast, were cultivated far earlier, at least as far back as the Babylonian garden of Merodach-baladan in 722–711 BCE.

Yet even in ancient Rome vegetable snobs oppressed cabbage fans. Pliny the Elder recounts that Apicius rejected young cabbage sprouts, causing young Drusus to follow suit, even though his father, Tiberius Caesar, scolded him for being 'so over-nice' – that is, fussy and snobbish. The Roman poet Ovid reinforced this notion that cabbage was food for poor folks. He recounts in his *Metamorphoses* how Baucis and Philemon, a poor, virtuous elderly couple, were visited by Jupiter and Hermes on a whim. They fed the disguised gods the best meal they could muster on short notice: boiled cabbage with a tiny strip of salt pork on top. Given that Baucis and Philemon's house was 'a homely shed; the roof, not far from ground, was thatch'd with reeds, and straw, together bound', they weren't exactly serving up caviar and champagne. No one was too poor to eat cabbages. In return for the couple's hospitality, Jupiter turned them into 'intertwining' trees, not cabbage.

Many authors have questioned just what exactly the Romans meant when they mentioned 'cabbage sprouts' (*caulic-auli*). In Diocletian's sixth edict (301 CE), a 'bundle' of cabbage sprouts is priced the same as five best-quality cabbages, or ten second-quality cabbages. Some authors have claimed the 'sprouts' are actually broccoli, but there is little evidence for that.

Some writers have cited the wild cabbages growing along English cliffs as evidence that cabbage has grown in Britain since the time of the Celts. However, it is much more likely that these rank little plants are descendants of imported cabbages. Ancient Greek authors noted that domesticated cabbages quickly reverted to scraggly little leaves if left to breed with local wild brassicas. Athenaeus' third-century BCE book *The Deipnosophistae* (The Dinner Table Philosophers) describes several evocative ways that cabbage could devolve: 'Seed brought from Rhodes to Alexandria produces a cabbage which is sweet for the first year, but after that period it becomes acclimatized.' Nicander says in the *Georgics*:

> Smooth-skinned is the cabbage, but sometimes it occurs in wild state, with many leaves, and grows rank in seeded gardens; either branching in curly tendrils with brownish leaves, or purplish and like disordered hair, or again, in ugly greenish tints its hollow leaf is like the sole-leather with which they mend sandals turned and patched; it is the plant which those of yore called the prophet among vegetables.

Korean farmers in the twelfth century also had to get seed from far away – in this case, Chinese cabbage growers in Beijing to keep growing pure-bred brassicas. The problem persisted for centuries: in his *Théâtre d'agriculture* (1600), Olivier de Serres said that green cabbage would degenerate, and that farmers needed to get new seed each year from Spain and Italy – Tortosa, Savona and Briançon. Gregor Mendel's explanations of genetic hybridization in the nineteenth century did not come a moment too soon.

In early modern Europe, cabbage acquired a mythic lineage. In his sixteenth-century satirical work *The Life of Gargantua and of Pantagruel*, Rabelais invented a much-quoted story about cabbage's Greek beginnings. When confronted with two

Caules onati.

Caules onati. complo. cala. mp. ficca in z. Electio recentes tenerores ao citinum. uura minum apiunt opilancos. Nocumentum ledunt uisecta. Remotio nocumin ai multo oleo. Quid gnar: sanguine malum. convenunt calidis inuentbz breme plus omnibz regionibz.

Cabbage harvest from the 15th-century *Tacuinum sanitatis.*

conflicting prophecies, Zeus thought so hard he sweated cabbages onto the ground, Rabelais wrote. In the classical versions of this tale, however, Zeus solves the paradox of the dog Laelaps, who always catches his prey, and the Teumessian fox, which could never be caught, by simply turning them into stone. The cabbages were a bit of Rabelaisian whimsy.

European cabbage soldiered through the ages. Cabbage's shifting identity makes it difficult to track exactly when and how modern headed cabbage spread to Europe and Asia, and it isn't clear exactly how these cold-adapted plants spread to the north even though they were known during Roman times. The Romans had headed cabbage, but it is hard to find any mention of the heads in Europe prior to the fourteenth-century English recipe collection *The Forme of Cury*, which mentions that 'caboches' are quartered for soup. It is hard to imagine quartering a bunch of kale. In Elizabethan England, the term 'cabbage' referred to the head, while the whole plant was called cabbage-cole or colewort – and colewort could refer to cabbage, or collards or kale. In Turkey in 1502, the Bursa Edict of Standards issued by Emperor Bayezıd ıı set the price of cabbage as one *akça* for four *okes* – the same price as carrots, watermelons and salt.

Sixteenth-century Dutch and Flemish painters were enamoured of cabbages, and they frequently featured in paintings with title descriptors such as 'vegetable stall'. A botanist who reviewed sixteenth-century Dutch paintings found that 'white' cabbages outnumbered cauliflowers by a ratio of four to one; no kale was found. Reviews of food transportation and market regulations for the time show that just a few vegetables dominated the Dutch market supply: cabbage, turnips, carrots,

Pieter Aertsen, *Market Scene*, 1569, oil on panel.

parsnips, onions, garlic, leeks and parsley. Cabbages show up in lusty situations in these paintings. Women vegetable-sellers have their breasts grabbed while displaying cabbages upturned to show a nipple-like root; a painting by Jacob Jordaens shows a mother pointing to turnips suggestively arranged around a cabbage while her half-naked toddler son lounges in the corner. Artists did not invent this association: children came *uyt den kool*, or 'out of a cabbage', in seventeenth-century Dutch literature, and were likely found there for a long time beforehand.

Chinese Cabbage and Beyond

Cabbages are rampant cross-breeders, and have caused farmers from Italy to Korea who lived near wild brassicas to complain about having to buy hybrid seed from distant merchants for more than a millennium. The sheer variety of brassicas makes it difficult to summarize the uses of cabbage in Chinese culture, where it appears that any and all cabbage variants are immensely popular. They include *Brassica juncea* mustard cabbages (*chieh-ts'ai*), *Brassica oleracea* var. *alboglabra* (Chinese kale, *chieh-lan-ts'ai*), *Brassica rapa pekinensis* (napa cabbage, *pai-ts'ai*) and *Brassica chinensis* (bok choy, *pai-ts'ai*), as well as good-old headed *Brassica oleracea* green cabbage. Bok choy and mustard cabbage grow best in China's south, while napa cabbage, like Western cabbage, is a cool-weather crop of the north. Some kind of cabbage is generally available in any season, although in truly overwhelming heat, residents of central and south China sometimes resort to water spinach or 'swamp cabbage' (*Ipomoea aquatica*), which is not a cabbage at all, but a relative of sweet potatoes (*Ipomoea batatas*). A survey from the 1920s of low-income families in Beijing found that napa cabbage alone accounted for a quarter of their spending on vegetables.

Chinese or napa cabbage took a long time to penetrate the West. The botanists at Kew Gardens started growing specimens in 1888, but trial gardeners beyond Kew over the next three decades had mixed opinions: one correspondent wrote that it had 'great value and was excellent as a late autumn salad – white, crisp, and sharp as the best summer cos lettuce', while another wrote, 'from a European standpoint no variety of Chinese Cabbage is worth growing being so very inferior in flavour to our own.'

Europeans have preferred to compose variations on just a few *Brassica* themes rather than exploring the cacophony of leafy cabbage diversity. Broccoli's name derives from the Italian *brocco* and the Latin *brachium*, meaning 'arm' or 'branch'. There

Cross-section of bok choy (*Brassica chinensis*).

is considerable debate over whether the *cyma* so often described by ancient Romans referred to something like broccoli, or cabbage shoots, or some other kind of young, tender *Brassica* entirely. The first reliably documented description of it was given by the French herbalist Jacques Daléchamps in his *Historia generalis plantarum* (1586). Some eighteenth-century English works refer to it as 'Italian asparagus', while others call it 'black broccoli' to distinguish it from white or cauliflower-broccoli. There are references to *borecoles* in both Dutch and English books by the eighteenth century as well, but that term refers to various kales.

Cauliflower is also a young upstart. Based on its genetic make-up, scientists have concluded that it is merely one single gene mutation away from being broccoli – rather as Dr Jekyll is a mere potion away from turning into Mr Hyde. The earliest known description of something that is certainly cauliflower – and not some odd form of broccoli – comes from the agricultural textbook *Kitab al-Felahah* (Book of Agriculture) of 1140, by Yahya ibn Muhammad Ibn-al-Awam, a Moorish Spaniard who named it variously as Syrian cabbage, Mosul cabbage or *quarnabit*, which is the current Arabic word for cauliflower. Something that sounds suspiciously like cauliflower also appears in the *Kitab al-Tabikh* (Baghdad Cookery Book), compiled in 1226, which features 'white cabbage'. In 1583 the Flemish botanist Rembert Dodoens was the first European to record the hot new vegetable trend, calling cauliflower *Brassica cypria*, or the cabbage from Cyprus. By 1633 the 'Cole-florey' was prominently featured in an expanded edition of John Gerard's *Herball*.

Brussels sprouts probably developed in the fourteenth century, near – surprise! – Brussels, and were supposedly served at the royal wedding feast of Alcande de Brederode in 1481, also in Brussels.

Brassica crops in the Americas generally arrived with Europeans. Although there are brassicas native to the Americas, they are cultivated for their roots, not their leaves, and historically have not been popular foodstuffs. The most prominent American cabbage relative is *Lepidium meyenii*, popularly known as maca, a root vegetable that is dried after harvest to reduce its load of pungent chemicals called glucosinolates. Maca was

Broccoli (*Brassica oleracea* var. *italica*) arranged for supermarket display.

'White Cabbage
Cole', from John
Gerard's *Herball*
(1644).

**4 *Braſſica capitata alba*.
White Cabbage Cole.**

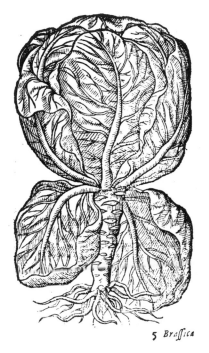

5 *Braſſica*

not terribly popular prior to the last two decades; there is very
little evidence that it was cultivated beyond the area around
Lake Junín, Peru, until the latter half of the twentieth century.
In the 1980s, total worldwide maca cultivation had dwindled
to 150 hectares (370 acres). One researcher noted that most
maca novices find maca rather repulsive. The reviled roots
became abruptly popular after modern marketers began to
advertise it as a cure-all for increased energy, women's men-
strual issues and as a 'natural alternative to Viagra'. Variously
diluted decoctions are available in supermarkets throughout
the developed world.

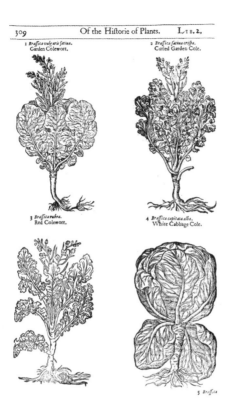

1 *Braſſica vulgaris ſativa.*
Garden Colewort.

2 *Braſſica ſativa criſpa.*
Curled Garden Cole.

3 *Braſſica rubra.*
Red Colewort.

4 *Braſſica capitata alba.*
White Cabbage Cole.

5 *Braſſica*

'Colewoorts',
from John
Gerard's *Herball*
(1644).

Cabbage (Not)

There are many other plants called 'cabbage' which really are
not cabbage at all. Skunk cabbage (*Symplocarpus foetidus*) is a
common plant of North American wetlands; it may be edible,
but very few people would try it, as its flowers and leaves
genuinely stink – attracting pollinating flies in the process.

Sub-Antarctic islands host plants sailors called Macquarie
Island cabbage (*Stilbocarpa polaris*) and Kerguelen cabbage
(*Pringlea antiscorbutica*). As the Kerguelen plant's name *antiscor-
butica* implies, these plants were cooked and eaten by seamen

on long ocean voyages to prevent scurvy. They worked, too, but opinions on the culinary qualities of these quasi-cabbages were mixed. Fabian von Bellingshausen, who circumnavigated Antarctica in 1821, wrote of Macquarie Island cabbage:

> The roots resemble cabbage in flavour. The sealers scrape the stalks and roots, cut them up very fine and make soup of them. We took a lot of these cabbages with us and preserved them for the use of the crew, the roots being pickled for the officers' mess. From the preserved cabbage we made a very tasty shchi [Russian cabbage soup], and we were sorry that we had not prepared more.

A century later, J. Inches Thomson wrote that Macquarie Island cabbage was 'a combination of parsnip and cabbage,

Skunk cabbage, aka *Symplocarpus foetidus*.

Illustration of Kerguelen cabbage from Joseph Dalton Hooker, *The Botany of the Antarctic Voyage of* HM *Discovery Ships 'Erebus' and 'Terror' in the Years 1839–1843* (1844).

and not particularly palatable'. The British botanist Joseph Dalton Hooker voyaged to the Antarctic from 1839 to 1843, and wrote of Kerguelen cabbage:

> To a crew long confined on salt provisions, or indeed to human beings under any circumstances, this is a most important vegetable, for it possesses all the essentially good qualities of its English namesake, whilst from its containing a great abundance of essential oil, it never produces heartburn or any of those disagreeable sensations which our pot-herbs are apt to do . . . The root tastes like horse-radish, and the young leaves or hearts resemble in flavor coarse mustard and cress. For one hundred and thirty days our crews required no fresh vegetable but

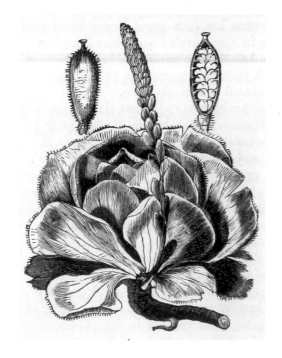

Kerguelen cabbage, from an 1850 book by J. Nunn.

Kerguelen cabbage, aka *Pringlea ascorbutica*.

this, which was for nine weeks regularly served out with the salt beef or pork, during which time there was no sickness on board.

The Frenchman Raymond Rallier du Baty, who lived at Kerguelen at various times from 1907 to 1914, reported,

> We gathered a good deal of this plant and made use of it in our cooking because we had a great need of vegetable food to keep our blood pure. But the Kerguelen cabbage is not an ideal green-stuff. We had to boil it twice before we could eat it, for it has a most rank and bitter taste, very much like the most powerful horse-radish. In the first boiling the water becomes of a dark yellow colour, but in the second boiling it is fairly clear and the cabbage then

becomes eatable. We made sauces with it, and chopped it up with our tinned meats for the stew-pot.

Would these gentlemen have persisted in experimenting with such a repulsive food if its unfurling leaves had not looked like run-of-the-mill garden cabbage?

2

The Cabbage of Fact and Dreams

Cabbage has always been a medicine for the body and the soul. Sauerkraut's vitamin C kept Captain Cook's sailors swabbing the decks in the 1760s while other ships' crews were collapsing with scurvy, and modern doctors prescribe cabbage-leaf poultices to soothe nursing mothers' engorged breasts. Before the discovery of vitamins made eating a contest between knowledge and desire, cabbage was eaten by ancient Greek women after childbirth to ward off witchcraft, and by Romans to cure anything at all.

There is a chemical basis for most (not all) of cabbage's medicinal effects, but cabbage's powers extend beyond the body. Cabbage leaves eaten on New Year's Day bring wealth in the new year in the American South. Babies have been found 'under a cabbage leaf' in Germany, the Netherlands and Belgium for hundreds of years. Like a witch's broom or Rumple-stiltskin's spinning wheel, a cabbage is a common, almost forgettable object with enormous magical potency.

Cabbage of Fact and Farm

Cabbage is a nutritious, adaptable plant, fecund and prolific amid Mediterranean zephyrs and dreary Baltic drizzles alike. Alaskans grow cabbages weighing up to 62 kg (138 lb), although a proud Yukon reporter admitted that these freakish vegetables are 'useless from a commercial standpoint'. Cabbages are a cool-weather crop, thriving at temperatures ranging from 15–20°C (60–68°F), but they will continue growing at temperatures down to 5°C (41°F), and young cabbage plants can withstand temperatures down to −12°C (10°F) for a night or two.

There are a few good records on medieval or ancient methods of growing cabbage. Part of the problem is nomenclature: in some countries, such as Sweden, the word for cabbage (*kål*) referred to any plant with green edible leaves, from lettuce to turnips. That might be because cabbage is extremely easy to grow. Bred from weeds, it sprouts readily for home gardeners and industrial farmers alike, and doesn't need any particular fertilizer, day length or temperature to thrive. There is also some evidence that it was so common that officials didn't bother keeping track of how or where it was grown. As historian Anon C. Zeven comments,

> Many archival records report cabbages, leek and onion and a few other vegetables for the Netherlands . . . These crops must have been grown in vegetable gardens, but in these records such gardens are not described and rarely mentioned.

A similar problem presented in Gdansk, Poland: 'For the 14th century . . . *Brassica oleracea* (cabbage), *B. rapa* (turnip) and *Pastinaca sativa* (parsnip), which were present in [preserved] botanical samples, were not mentioned in the documents from then.' What little success archivists have had in determining how cabbages were grown has come from paintings, such as Pieter Breugel the Elder's *The Tower of Babel*, painted circa 1563, which features an urban cabbage garden near its centre.

Burpee's Farm Annual (1882): an illustration of typical types of headed cabbage.

Detail of cabbage yard (left centre, behind wall) from Pieter Bruegel the Elder, *The Tower of Babel*, 1563, oil on oak panel.

One of the few exceptions is a volume titled *The Feat of Gardening* (1440), authored by one Master John. His section on worts – a catch-all phrase for any type of leafy brassica, cabbage, kale or collards – begins with the epigram: 'Worts we must have / Both to master and knave.' Master John goes on to detail how to grow worts, which were not harvested like modern cabbage. Instead of providing a tidy head to be lopped off once in the autumn, these worts were grown to have leaves gathered periodically through the season. For that reason, Master John declared that it was important to sow the crop several times in May, July, November and March. Young worts could be plucked just six weeks after planting, while modern headed cabbages need at least two months to mature. However, once cabbage has matured, there is no rush to pick it; unlike strawberries or young lettuce, a mature cabbage is a solid, stalwart vegetable, and can be left in the field for an extended period before being picked and stored, as long as it does not freeze solid – an advantage when the supply of farm workers is low.

E. Phillips Fox, *The Cabbage Patch*, 1889, oil on canvas.

Red cabbages were being grown in Germany by 1150 and in England by 1600. By the late nineteenth century, transportation allowed long-distance cabbage-trading. In the u.s., northern cabbage-growers would supply the South during the summer, while southern cabbage growers would send their cabbages northward in the early spring after the northerners had exhausted their winter supply. Today's farmers either direct-seed cabbage in places where the weather is particularly foul or put small transplants in the field in the early spring. Various cabbages are bred to resist cold, heat, insects, bacteria and fungal diseases.

Farmers don't have as many options as they once did. Many heirloom varieties have been lost as farming has been increasingly industrialized. In 1903, 544 different varieties of cabbage were available from u.s. seed companies; by 1983 just 28 of those varieties could be found at the u.s. National Seed Storage Laboratory (now the National Laboratory for Genetic Resources Preservation).

Today China leads the world in production of all brassicas, spawning more than 36 million metric tons of various cabbage stuffs in 2007, representing more than half of world cabbage production. European cabbage farmers, including those in Russia, collectively produced just over 12 million metric tons.

Cabbage for the Long Haul

Fresh cabbage lasts up to four months if stored in cellar conditions: just above freezing – that is, 1–2°C (30–36°F) – and with high humidity, outlasting all but the longest winters. For those months, there is sauerkraut, which can be stored for years. But this *Wundergemüse* is not as kind to diners as the equally versatile yet bland potato. Eaten raw, it provokes flatulence in effete stomachs; it tastes bitter to many epicures; and it stinks to high heaven if heated too long by neglectful cooks.

Our ingenious forebears, fond as they were of low-maintenance vegetables, developed methods to tame cabbages' most indelicate shortcomings, enabling them to eat more cabbage. They learned to tame cabbage by cooking, salting and fermenting, allowing them to eat more nutritious food for less effort, freeing them to spend their agricultural time on more finicky crops like wheat and rice, which contain more sugars, and can be fermented into alcohol. (Very few people attempt to make alcohol from cabbage, although there are persistent rumours that Jägermeister might consist primarily of cabbage juice.)

Cabbage's offensive elements fall into three categories: the bitterness, the windiness and the stink. Each of these nuisances is caused by a separate set of innate chemicals which protect cabbages from being devoured by caterpillars, weevils and Michelin-star-restaurant patrons.

Stink

The stench of cooked cabbage is legend; a quick web search reveals comparisons to sewage, urine, sweaty feet and women's genitalia. The metabolic disorder hypermethioninemia is diagnosed partly by a 'cabbage' smell in urine. What all these unpleasant experiences have in common are compounds which contain sulphur. In cabbage's case, there are several chemical culprits. The chief offender appears to be a chemical called dimethyl sulphide, which gives cooked cabbage, broccoli, cauliflower and – surprise! – okra their vegetal savour.

Dimethyl sulphide can have paradoxical effects depending on its concentration in a food. In small quantities, it does not necessarily taste like cabbage at all; it lends an unmistakable tinned-sweetcorn flavour to cooked corn, and provides 'complexity' in red wines in concentrations of up to 30 parts per billion. At concentrations higher than 50 parts per billion, 'complexity' turns back into 'cabbage', as though Cinderella's godmother's spell had just worn off your wine glass. Another sulphur compound, methyl thiobutanoate, contributes a flavour note to strawberries, even though it is described as 'cheesy, garlic, cabbage' when sampled alone in high concentrations.

Alas, when more than 45 parts per billion of dimethyl sulphide waft out of your soup pot, the compound 'contributes a highly undesirable "cooked vegetable" or "cabbage-like" malodor'. As Robert J. McGorrin observed in a study of volatile sulphur compounds in food, cabbage emits a moderate amount of dimethyl sulphide after ten minutes of boiling, but after ninety minutes it is 'excessive'. By contrast, mustardy allyl isothiocyanate peaks at about twenty minutes. The amount of these compounds varies within the head: outer leaves produce four times as much dimethyl sulphide and five times as much allyl isothiocyanate as the younger, innocent inner leaves.

Although scientists have investigated the content of cabbage-cooking fumes, they have not been terribly interested in figuring out how to dispel them. Perhaps food scientists don't spend much time cooking cabbage in their homes; perhaps industrial stew-making facilities have very weak unions, and workers simply put up with the stench.

Traditional European and North American solutions include:

> Cooking cabbage with caraway, bay leaf, a whole unshelled walnut, celery, vinegar, lemon juice, a piece of bread or a biscuit.

> Using lots of water and high heat to dilute the smell.

> Leaving a bowl of white vinegar next to the stove.

None of these solutions have been scientifically shown to have any effect whatsoever. Either cook your cabbage for less than twenty minutes, or don't cook it at all. One other way that actually works to reduce cabbage's smell is to slice it thinly and fry it in hot oil. The coating of oil on the surface diminishes the ability of the glucosinolates to waft into the air – and by the time the stuff has traversed the anaerobic cauldron of diners' stomachs, the compounds have been denatured into obscurity.

Bitterness

Raw cabbage's sharp, mustardy taste is the product of a class of chemicals called glucosinolates. Cabbages and their brassica kin appear to manufacture these tongue-irritating compounds because they help them to battle insects, disease and other plants. Glucosinolates reduce damage by mammals, birds, insects, bacteria, fungi, nematodes and some humans. But not *all* humans.

Some people are acutely sensitive to cabbage's bitter flavours, and some are not – not because they are ill-bred, or have numbed their tastebuds with cigarettes, or are just trying to torture their pernickety children. These people may not be able to detect a cabbage's bitter taste at all. A particular gene, TAS2R38, moderates sensitivity to these particular chemicals. People who carry the 'taster' or PAV version of the TAS2R38 gene taste glucosinolates in a range from bitter to unspeakably bitter. The lucky bearers of the AVI variation may blithely gulp their cabbage as though there were nothing sweeter on this earth . . . except that there is no single gene for taste, and other genes appear to rush in to assist in perceiving unpleasantness where TAS2R38 fails. But they still aren't as sensitive as the PAV tasters. About 5 per cent of tasters with yet another rare version of the TAS2R38 gene, called PAI, can detect the bitter chemical PTC – a stand-in for glucosinolates in taste experiments – in concentrations as low as 1 millimole per litre, while close to 30 per cent of AVI tasters cannot detect PTC until it reaches concentrations more than 4,000 times as high.

Worldwide, about 50 per cent of gourmands are PAV bearers, doomed to a life of bitterness, but among native populations in Central America the proportion of PAV 'tasters' rises to 100 per cent, while about two-thirds of people in some regions of Northern Europe are AVI 'non-tasters'.

What this means is that you cannot please everyone. In any given region, a certain number of people will declare that cabbage and its ilk are repulsive weeds only fit for horses and stingy Greek philosophers, while others will wonder aloud why their snobbish neighbours are foolishly rejecting a cheap, tasty food. Did Diogenes prefer cabbage because it cost so little, or because he simply could not taste its bitter sting?

Still, cabbages appear to have other motivations for producing glucosinolates besides irritating tender tongues. When glucosinolate compounds break down – through exposure to air by cutting, for example – one of the chemicals they produce is allyl isothiocyanate, which gives sharp, pungent, bitter and horseradish-like notes to raw cabbage. Cabbages also produce a certain amount of allyl isothiocyanate directly. Allyl isothiocyanate is so pungent and irritating – humans cannot stand concentrations in the air over 10 parts per million – that researchers filed a patent in 2011 to use its odour as a fire alarm for those who are blind and deaf.

Allyl isothiocyanate is also what plant scientists call an allelopathic compound; it discourages other plants from growing nearby by changing the surrounding soil. It is found in moderate concentrations (429 parts per million) in garlic mustard (*Alliaria petiolata*), a Eurasian garden herb that has escaped cultivation in North America, where it is considered invasive – partly due to its vegecidal tendencies. Brown mustard and horseradish, relatives in the Brassicaceae family, are awash in allyl isothiocyanate (approx. 12,000 and 2,600 parts per million), while cabbage leaves commonly carry a mere 20 parts per million. High concentrations of allyl isothiocyanate also inhibit the growth of yeasts and moulds and protect wild cabbages from some types of mildew.

However, this kind of chemical warfare is best left to the young and strong. The more recent growth in a cabbage's core has a far greater proportion of allyl isothiocyanate than the old, tired leaves – around 14–42 mg per kg for the pith versus 2–8 mg per kg for the leaves. Take your cabbage and ferment it – to make sauerkraut, kimchi, or curtido – and it loses heart, or at least its bitter compounds, which simply waft away. In general, cabbage which is fermented at a temperature of 19°C (66°F) will glycolyse away all the pesky allyl isothiocyanate within three days.

Cabbages and their brassica kin also increase their glucosinolate levels in response to a variety of stresses, including drought, high temperature, saline soil, UVB radiation, and soil that lacks nutrients. In short, if your cabbage is uncomfortable, you will be uncomfortable too.

Human predation of brassicas has recently increased thanks to reports that glucosinolates reduce the risk of cancer. But don't eat too much. Cabbage glucosinolates can interfere with a body's uptake of iodine, causing an enlarged thyroid gland (goitre) in humans, sheep and goats.

Wind

Cabbage's contribution to human aroma is not unique. Like dry beans, and lentils, asparagus, broccoli and Brussels sprouts, cabbage contains large quantities of a sort of sugar molecule (a trisaccharide if you're picky) called raffinose. This pernickety substance spurns the importunes of the stomach and small intestine, and doesn't get digested until it finally meets the large intestine, its destiny. There, ravenous bacteria break the raffinose into smaller sugars, creating methane gas – and flatulence – as a side effect.

But cabbage-eaters are not condemned to eternal flatulence. Raffinose is not a constant feature of cabbage. Both raffinose and sucrose concentrations increase in cabbage as it hardens at cold temperatures, protecting it from frost. As temperatures rise and cabbage de-hardens, preparing its soft tissues to grow, the amounts of raffinose and sucrose in the leaves decline sharply – in the case of raffinose, perhaps to zero. And thus, the paradox. The winter cabbage is far sweeter than the first shoots of spring, but also wreaks a rank revenge by causing increased farting at a time of year when people spend more time in confined environments. O, cruel cabbage!

Colour

Red cabbage is a well-known acid/base indicator, a staple of primary-school science laboratories (you generally do not have to worry about the students trying to eat the test materials). In the presence of alkaline materials, such as sodium bicarbonate, it turns blue. Cooks who are particularly bored can spend an afternoon transmuting cabbage from red to blue by alternately pouring vinegar and bicarbonate of soda into the cabbage pot. The end result will not be palatable, no matter what the hue.

Cabbage of Health

Cabbage has been credited with a confounding variety of cures – and a few of them actually work. Most of the Greeks' notions didn't, though. Theophrastus distinguished three types of cabbage in his *Historia plantarum* (Enquiry into Plants, *c.* 300 BCE): the curly leaved, the smooth-leaved, and the 'wild form' which had small round leaves, many branches and 'a sharp medicinal taste; wherefore physicians use it for the stomach.' Grape vines were less appreciative of cabbages' charms, sneering at its common, malodorous ways:

> the vine-shoot, whenever it comes near this plant, turns
> back and looks away, as though the smell were hostile

to it. Indeed Androkydes used this act as an example to demonstrate the use of cabbage against wine, to expel the fumes of drunkenness; or, said he, even when it is alive, the vine avoids the smell.

That alleged vegetal disdain was rooted in a particularly nasty act of revenge by Dionysus, the Greek god of wine and madness. Lycurgus, the king of Thrace, banned the cult of Dionysus, which was getting a bit too uppity for Thracian polite society. As might be expected, Dionysus drove Lycurgus mad. Lycurgus came to believe that his son was an ivy vine, and pruned him to death. The land grew barren, and an oracle declared that there would be no harvest unless Lycurgus was put to death. Bound for execution, Lycurgus wept in sorrow, and his tears became cabbages.

This notion that cabbages and grape vines cannot grow together still persists today, despite the complete lack of evidence that they have any effect on each other. A 2012 article in the *San Francisco Gate* tries to back up this claim, weakly: 'Never plant . . . greens, such as lettuce (*Lactuca sativa*) and cabbage (*Brassica oleracea var. capitata*) or garlic (*Allium sativum*), next to grapes . . . planting those vegetables near your grape vines will result in stunted growth, often due to high water requirements.'

Thanks to this veggie war, the ancient Greeks reasoned, cabbage could disarm grapes' most fearsome power: the hangover. Athenaeus' third-century CE *Deipnosophistae*, also known as *The Dinner Table Philosophers*, claims with just as much sincerity as you would expect from a dinner table philosopher that Egyptians serve cabbages first at their banquets because they want to get drunk, and that many people add cabbage seeds to hangover cures. However, he follows this very serious information with a series of quotes from Greek comedies,

44

Johann Georg Seitz, *Vegetable Still-life with Rabbits*, 1870, oil on wood. Note the kohlrabis, lower right.

such as 'Woman, you must think I am a cabbage, for you try to shift all your headache upon me, so I believe.'

It is unclear if Athenaeus' dinner table philosophers took cabbage's powers seriously. Later in the *Dinner*, he also notes that cabbage is used as the rough equivalent of 'Gosh golly!' among passionate characters in comedies. He fills the page with quotes like 'So help me Cabbage!', taken from Epicharmus' *Earth and Sea* and Eupolis' *The Bathers*. In reality, the Egyptians may well have got the idea for serving cabbages at drinking parties from the Greeks, as there is strong evidence that the Greeks brought cabbage to Egypt.

The Greek physician Dioscorides and Roman politician Cato credited cabbage with curing pretty much every human malady. Disocorides, a Greek doctor who served the Roman army, credited *Krambe emeros*, or wild cabbage, with curing snakebite, gangrene and freckles, among other things. In his *De agricultura* (On Agriculture, *c.* 160 BCE), Cato the Elder credits cabbage with curing wounds, colic, diseases of the digestive tract and urinary tract, ulcers, arthritis, insomnia, swollen spleens . . . the list goes on and on.

By the tenth century, Rome's wonders were diminished, but cabbage's glory shone on in the *Geoponika*. This agricultural textbook was compiled from a swarm of classical sources in Constantinople for the Byzantine emperor Constantine VII Porphyrogennetos, and devotes an entire chapter to 'Cabbage and its Medicinal Powers', which include curing phthisis, jaundice, distemper, leprosy, 'the itch', gout, inflamed tonsils, dog bites, insomnia and weak vision, making children 'grow very fast' and counteracting poisonous mushrooms.

Interestingly, the *Geoponika*'s author also mentions that 'Old cabbage seed will produce the *raphanus*' – that is, a turnip, or at least something with smaller, less tasty leaves. Athenaeus also mentioned that cabbages grown in Alexandria were delightful the first year, but bitter the second year, 'due to the acrid influence of the soil', so Alexandrians took to importing their seeds from Rhodes. Although this explanation may have suited Rhodes's seed merchants, the transformation was probably due to the hybrid Rhodes cabbages cross-pollinating with local wild brassicas, producing wayward offspring. Cabbages originated in northern Africa, and there were plenty of feral brassicas to serve as a bad influence on any innocent young cabbage that might cross their paths.

The *Geoponika* also repeats the old canard that cabbage is a fine cure for drunkenness. However, in the next sentence, the author says that you won't get drunk if you chant 'Thrice thundered Jupiter from Ida's heights.' Eating raw cabbage is not a folk cure so much as another type of magic spell. It is about as helpful to most readers as the *Geoponika*'s recommendation to sow cabbage seeds in February, a month when Swedish growers would have a hard time even finding their garden beds under the snow.

Abu Marwan Abd al-Malik Ibn Zuhr, the twelfth-century Moorish Spanish physician known as Avenzoar to Europeans, took a dimmer view of cabbage in his *Kitab al-Agdiya waladwiya* (Book on Foodstuffs and Drugs), writing:

> People eat cabbage and extol its praises even though it is the worst of all vegetables as it creates black bile, susceptible minds, leprosy, revolting scabies, and epilepsy. I am not familiar with any vegetable that is worse than this one, with the exception of aubergine (eggplant), which is fairly similar. It is warm and dry and has no recognized beneficial property with one exception; whether eaten raw or cooked it clears up one's throat in an extraordinary and marvellous way.

The twelfth-century Arab-Hispano cookbook *Kitab al-Tabikh* paired caraway with cabbage because 'it improves the delicacy, gives it flavour, and releases the vegetable gases.' Whether 'vegetable gases' means cabbage's cooking odour or postprandial farting is difficult to say.

All these ideas persisted through the ages, with variations. *The Four Seasons of the House of Cerruti*, composed in fourteenth-century Italy, suggests using cooked cabbage juice mixed with honey as eyedrops to improve weak vision. Sixteenth-century French physicians also had an expansive view of cabbages' medicinal properties. In the 1570s Antoine Mizauld wrote in his book *The Medicinal Garden Enriched with Many Diverse Remedies and Secrets*, 'The juice of raw cabbage sipped with wine serves as a remedy against vipers' bites; and as a plaster with fenugreek flour is a sovereign remedy against gout and other diseases of the joints.'

Karl Hartmann, *Autumn Sun*, 1903, oil on canvas.

Robert Burton gives paradoxical accounts of cabbage in his *Anatomy of Melancholy* (1621), claiming that 'Amongst herbs to be eaten I find gourds cucumbers coleworts melons disallowed but especially cabbage. It causeth troublesome dreams and sends up black vapours to the brain . . . it brings heaviness to the soul.' But later on, Burton lists 'half-boiled cabbage' in his catalogue of purgers of black bile, that is, the mysterious humour that was supposed to cause depression in the first place. Perhaps Burton was one of the super-tasters, doomed to ruminate on bitterness with every bite of a brassica.

Cabbage's Melancholy Juice

Other seventeenth-century British authors were more dubious about cabbage's charms. In his *Acetaria* (1699), his book about salads, John Evelyn wrote,

> Cabbage, Brassica (and its several kinds) Pompey's beloved Dish, so highly celebrated by old Cato, Pythagoras, and Chrysippus the Physician (as the only Panacea) is not so generally magnify'd by the rest of Doctors, as affording but a crass and melancholy Juice . . . which makes me wonder at the Veneration we read the Ancients had for them, calling them Divine, and swearing, *per Brassicam*.

(Evelyn clearly took Athenaeus' 'So help me cabbage!' a little too seriously.)

Nineteenth-century Americans were suspicious of cabbage – and every other vegetable, truth be told. Until twentieth-century scientists discovered vitamins, cookbook writers and home economists didn't see any point to vegetables other than promoting intestinal transit, and cabbage and its fellow vegetables were treated as edible toxic waste. Eliza Leslie recommended in 1851 that cabbage be boiled for two hours before it was deemed edible – long enough to allow glucosinolates to permeate and perfume the drapery, to be sure. In a 1910 edition of Mrs E. E. Kellogg's *Science in the Kitchen*, it was recommended to boil young cabbage for one hour, and older cabbages for three hours. Conventional opponents to the Rev.

Sylvester Graham's radical vegetarian precepts claimed that his followers found 'long life in starvation [and] moral reform in bran and cabbage.'

Cabbage may not guarantee moral reform, but it does have plenty of soluble and insoluble fibre, calcium, potassium, folate, carotenoids and lutein – and vitamin C. One of the few medical conditions for which cabbage is a genuine, proven remedy is scurvy, a deadly deficiency of vitamin C and a common scourge of sailors who go months without fresh fruit or vegetables on long sea voyages. Captain James Cook, an explorer and captain in the British Royal Navy, tried sauerkraut (or, as he wrote in his journals, 'Sour Kroutt') on his lengthy voyages of 1768–80 to stave off scurvy, the deadly sailor-killing syndrome.

Cook really had no idea how sauerkraut might prevent scurvy, and also attempted to stave off the disease by feeding his crew malt, 'portable soup', vinegar, mustard and rob (concentrated boiled orange and lemon juice) on his voyages, and took on fresh fruits, greens and extraordinary quantities of onions. However, in 1768 Cook requisitioned enough sauerkraut for 'a proportion for twelve months for seventy men [to] be sent aboard at the rate of two pounds per man per week' – enough to supply 150 mg (0.005 oz) of ascorbic acid to every crewman – and he was determined that his crew would eat it. The seamen refused to swallow their allotted cabbagey goodness until Captain Cook made a large show of putting a great pile of sauerkraut on the cabin table where the ship's officers dined each day. As Cook put it,

> whatever you give them out of the Common way . . . you will hear nothing but murmurings gainest the man that first invented it; but the Moment they see their Superiors set a Value upon it, it becomes the finest stuff in the World.

Cook even planted some cabbage seeds in New Zealand, in the hope he would find plants when he returned.

Cabbage leaves have also been used as poultices for wounds since ancient times – originally perhaps because the leaves are simply a convenient size and shape. In the United Kingdom and Ireland, the leaves have been used as a wrap for rheumatism (Cornwall), ulcers (Ireland), headaches (Essex), boils and abscesses (Shropshire, Cheshire, East Anglia) and eczema (Scotland). Portraitist Mary Lyde Hicks Williams, whose subjects were African Americans in post-Civil War North Carolina, painted a woman with a collard-green leaf tied around her head, 'for headache', in around 1900.

Cabbages and other brassicas are surprisingly good sources of calcium, a mineral more often associated with milk and salmon bones. Unlike other green vegetables, the gentle brassicas are low in both oxalic and phytic acids, which bind with calcium and block its absorption. While a typical human can absorb only 5 per cent of the calcium in spinach, a whopping 61 per cent of the calcium in broccoli is absorbed – twice the rate of milk and dairy products (30 per cent). A typical cup of whole milk with 276 mg of calcium should yield 14 mg of usable calcium, while a cup of raw cabbage with 33 mg of calcium should yield close to 20 mg of usable calcium. That said, many Westerners will drink a cup of milk, but eschew chewing their way through a cup of raw cabbage, rendering the cabbage's calcium unusable after all.

In the late twentieth century, there was a flurry of research into cabbage and other brassicas' alleged ability to prevent cancer. Results have been ambiguous. The problem is that people who eat more cabbage also eat more of every other sort of vegetable as well – solanums, legumes, alliums – so it is hard to detect a protective effect of cabbage alone. Cabbage's power to prevent some cancers – chiefly gastric cancer and

Christ, borne aloft on two cabbage leaves, from the *Hortus deliciarum*, 'The Garden of Delights', a manuscript prepared in the Hohenburg Abbey in Alsace in 1185.

lung cancer – seems to depend on an individual's genetic make-up and their ability to excrete glucosinolates quickly, and there is even some evidence that eating large quantities of brassicas can increase tumour growth in some people. In short, you don't have to eat your broccoli to stay healthy if you don't want to.

Cabbage has a curious relationship to sexuality. Its leaves and seeds have been used since antiquity as contraceptives and abortifacients. Many classical writers including Dioscorides wrote that cabbage leaves and flowers could act as oral contraceptives, and repeated the Roman Pliny the Elder's claim that cabbage seeds can cause sterility. The Arabic physician

Ibn Sina (Avicenna), born around 980 CE, recommended cabbage leaves and seeds in suppositories and as a sort of fibrous cervical cap. Yet cabbage has also long been a friend to women. Today in the U.S., Europe and India nursing mothers are encouraged to put cabbage leaves in their bras to soothe painful, milk-engorged breasts, though medical studies show that cabbage is not any more effective than a cool gel pack.

In Renaissance Europe, cabbage was also seen as an aphrodisiac. Cabbage's flatulence-inducing 'wind' was supposed to be able to bloat or inflate all the extremities of the body – including the genitals. Beans and some root vegetables were included in this category as well. It is unclear how the cabbage-eater was supposed to attract a romantic partner amid all that farting. Perhaps cabbage's sexy reputation is why American and European parents have been telling their gullible children for centuries that they came from under a cabbage leaf.

Cabbage of Dreams

Cabbage has always loomed large in the imagination – especially the Jersey cabbage, or walking-stick kale, which grows a thick stem up to 3 m (10 ft) tall, and may have inspired the story of Jack and the Beanstalk (or, rather, Jack and the Kalestalk). For some reason, cabbage is also a centre of odd holiday traditions. On Halloween in Scotland, nineteenth-century revellers would 'burn the reekie mehr' – create a torch by taking a cabbage or kale stalk, hollowing out the middle, and filling it with straw to blow smoke into their neighbours' houses through the keyhole. Cabbage also served as a Halloween fortune-telling device. In a footnote to his poem 'Halloween' (1785), Robert Burns described a Scottish holiday custom:

The first ceremony of Halloween is pulling each a 'stock', or plant of kail. They must go out, hand in hand, with eyes shut, and pull the first they meet with: its being big or little, straight or crooked, is prophetic of the size and shape of the grand object of all their spells – the husband or wife.

One shudders to think what conclusion a young lady would come to if she grasped a walking-stick kale.

The tradition of Halloween cabbage fortune-telling was also reported in northern Ireland in 1835, and at some point made a leap to the Americas. The night before Halloween is still called 'Cabbage Night' in parts of New England and New Jersey – and pranksters took their Brassicaceae seriously. Writing about Cabbage Night in the 1930s in Framingham, Massachusetts, one author remarked that the night's name originated in the Scottish fortune-telling tradition, because

> Once the cabbage had served its purpose, the only logical thing to do with it was throw it against the door and run

Jersey cabbage, or 'walking-stick kale'.

Antique Halloween postcard from 1912 by Elizabeth Clapsaddle featuring cabbages and Scottish tartan, perhaps reflecting Scottish Halloween fortune-telling traditions.

"O, is my true love tall and grand? O, is my sweetheart bonny?"

HALLOWE'EN

really fast, thus beginning a long tradition of Halloween pranks. Framingham teens skipped the fortune-telling and stuck with vegetable-throwing, adding it to their already large repertoire of tricks.

In Halifax, Nova Scotia, and some maritime areas of New England the title is 'Cabbage Stump Night', as tricksters used cabbage stalks to bother their neighbours by banging on their doors.

Many curious cabbage traditions are recorded in nineteenth-century folklore collections of dubious origin. According to one, in Finistère, France, pulling cabbages on St Stephen's day (26 December) was frowned upon as St Stephen was supposed

White cabbage in Sonsbeck, Germany.

to have been stoned to death in a cabbage patch. Another repeats a story from the Havel region of northeastern Germany, a variation on the mâche-stealing exploits of Rapunzel:

> One Christmas Eve a peasant felt a great desire to eat cabbage and, having none himself, he slipped into a neighbour's garden to cut some. Just as he had filled his basket, the Christ-Child rode past on his white horse, and said: 'Because thou hast stolen on the holy night, thou shalt immediately sit in the moon with thy basket of cabbage.'

The culprit was immediately wafted skyward, becoming the man in the moon.

Some African American spiritualist churches also used cabbages as a sort of magical device. In the 1950s in Nashville, Tennessee, Bishop Wilma Stewart would lead 'cabbage demonstrations', blessing cabbages for her congregation. Every year, on 24 November, members of the church would bring cabbages to be blessed; some devotees in other southern and Midwestern states would send cabbages to the church through the post. The cabbages were returned to their owners, and three days later the congregants would eat their cabbages before sunset. Every time they ate the cabbage, they would ask for a blessing – a new car, money or luck in love. Throughout the American South, eating cabbage (or collards, or kale) on New Year's Day is supposed to bring money in the coming year, and the Pennsylvania Dutch (actually, Americans of German descent) eat sauerkraut for good luck in the new year.

Cabbage has more ancient celestial associations as well. In the *Hortus deliciarum* (The Garden of Delights), a manuscript prepared in the Hohenburg Abbey in Alsace in 1185, an illustration of the genealogy of Christ shows him borne aloft between two cabbage leaves. This is probably due to a play on words: the Hebrew name for 'cabbage', *keruv* (כורכ), is identical to that for 'cherub'. That angelic identity is one explanation for why modern Ashkenazi Jews eat cabbage rolls on Simchat Torah, the holiday that celebrates the end of the annual cycle of Torah readings and the beginning of a new liturgical year. According to the Book of Exodus, two cherubs (cabbages?) were supposed decorations on the cover of the Ark of the Covenant, which held the Ten Commandments. More prosaically, the Hebrew words in a prayer said for the preceding week of Sukkot, *Kol Mevasser* (רשבמ לוק, the Herald), sound to German and Yiddish speakers very much like the phrase *Kohl mit Wasser*, or cabbage with water. (The cabbage must be boiled before it is rolled; otherwise, you just have cabbage flats.) Some Jewish communities eat cabbage soup for similar reasons. The cabbage rolls themselves are supposed to look like Torah scrolls when placed side by side.

Cabbages are also harbingers of death and war. North Carolina folklore claims that if a cabbage seeds in its first year, there will be a death in the family. The medieval Welsh physicians of Myddfai wrote, 'If you wish to die, eat cabbages in August.' A Greek proverb states that 'Cabbage served twice is death,' although it is probably more of an objection to leftovers than a true warning. In 1688 the New England Puritan cleric Cotton Mather encountered a cabbage with branches 'exactly resembling' a rapier, a cutlass and a club, which he took as a sign that war with the Native Americans was imminent. It is hard to imagine just how a modern cabbage can produce anything remotely resembling a cutlass, but Mather was a man of God, not botany.

In the nineteenth century, cabbages found their place in the sun, culturally speaking, when Charles Dodgson, otherwise known as Lewis Carroll, included them in a line in the hallucinatory poem 'The Walrus and the Carpenter' in *Through the Looking-glass and What Alice Found There*, his 1871 sequel to *Alice's Adventures in Wonderland*. The twins Tweedledum and Tweedledee recite this poem, a sordid tale of a talking walrus and a carpenter leading innocent young bipedal oysters on a fatal walk along the seashore. Midway through the poem, the walrus stops on a rock, and begins to speak:

'The time has come,' the Walrus said,
'To talk of many things:
Of shoes – and ships – and sealing-wax –
Of cabbages – and kings –
And why the sea is boiling hot –
And whether pigs have wings.'

Carroll's pairing of kings and lowly cabbage turned out to be extremely useful for editors casting about for titles.

John Tenniel's illustration of 'The Walrus and the Carpenter', a poem by
Lewis Carroll in *Through the Looking-glass and What Alice Found There* (1871).

Books, short stories, and articles in newspapers, magazines
and academic journals have all filched the phrase. By contrast,
the mundane, workaday 'shoes and ships and sealing wax'
waits forlornly for similar attention.

3
The Older the Better

Raw cabbage can remain palatable for up to four months in a cellar before putrid liquefaction begins – but take that same head and drown it in salted water and you can create an everlasting vegetable zombie, the cabbage undead. Food scientists have found that fermented vegetables become 'microbiologically stable' if all the sugars are fermented away, the jars are airtight and the liquid is sufficiently acidic. German sauerkraut, Korean kimchi and Chinese *xian cai* are all forms of fermented cabbage. The only quibble is whose fermented cabbage came first.

Fermentation is not the only way to store cabbage. It has been pickled in wine and dry-salted since ancient times, and there have been attempts made to preserve cabbage by drying it. Those attempts did not end happily. It was one of the vegetables the Union army dried into large slabs to feed the troops during the American Civil War, and the u.s. Army dried 'one hundred tons of cabbage a day' to send to Britain as part of a Lend-Lease food programme during the Second World War. Although in the years following both the Civil War and the Second World War new commercial food markets emerged in the u.s. – canned goods after the Civil War, freeze-dried convenience foods after the Second World War – private manufacturers did not flock to sell dried cabbage after either conflict. Perhaps twentieth-century consumers had the same experience as Mary T. S. Schäffer, an explorer who struck out for the Canadian Rockies in the 1880s with supplies for a lengthy expedition. Schäffer was not pleased with many of her supplies – the granulose extract was not as sweet as promised, the dried milk and eggs seemed to have evolved separately from farm animals – but she especially detested the cabbage, writing, 'For instance, beware of the dried cabbage; no fresh air in existence will ever blow off sufficient of the odor to let it get safely to the mouth.'

Chinese authors wrote about soured cabbage in the sixth century, and something like kimchi was described eight hundred years ago by the Korean poet Yi Kyu-bo, although kimchi's defining hot peppers did not appear until the Columbian Exchange. Salted cabbage was described by ancient Roman writers, but sauerkraut's origins in northern Europe are obscured by questionable legends about Genghis Khan importing pickled cabbage to Europe on horseback. Kimchi is so central to Korean meals that a poor napa cabbage harvest in 2010 provoked a 'kimchi crisis' throughout South Korea.

Today, sauerkraut is credited with miraculous healing powers thanks to the unregenerate bacteria lurking among the leaves. It is true that fermenting cabbage not only preserves vitamins A and C, but actually increases the cabbages' vitamin B content. However, sauerkraut and kimchi are not always benevolent. Despite the vitamins and glucosinolates, frequent consumption, in Korea and Japan, of salted, pickled food – including kimchi – increases the risk of gastric cancer. Fermented cabbage can also have high amounts of tyramine, which interferes with MAOI medications prescribed for mental illness. And despite the best efforts of millions of lactobacilli, and wishful thinking by German vegetarians, sauerkraut does not contain significant quantities of vitamin B12, a vitamin generated only by animals and a decidedly different set of bacteria from sauerkraut's fermenters.

Sauerkraut

Sauerkraut is credited to prehistoric German ingenuity, but the Germans were probably not the first people to appreciate sauerkraut's sour charms. The earliest surviving Chinese agricultural encyclopedia, the *Qimin Yaoshu*, a title variously translated as *Essential Ways of Living for the Common People* and *Essential Techniques for the Peasantry*, contains extensive instructions in

German white-cabbage sauerkraut, fermented and ready to eat.

Paul Kauffmann, *Making Choucroute*, 1902, illustration

sixth-century vegetable preservation techniques. (Presumably an 'Essential Techniques for Royalty' would cover different topics – say assassinations.) It mentioned 31 vegetables grown by Chinese farmers, including Chinese cabbage and contains an entire chapter on fermenting vegetables. According to the food historian Joyce Toomre, 40 per cent of these recipes are different versions of sauerkraut. Toomre proposes that sauerkraut was brought to Russia and Eastern Europe by the Tartars during the Mongol invasion of 1237, along with more elegant foodstuffs such as cinnamon and saffron. Yet the *Qimin Yaoshu* contains several other methods for preserving vegetables as well: keeping them in wine, cooked rice or vinegar.

It is not clear why sauerkraut won the day, although it preserves more vitamins than other methods, and for land-locked farmers it was much more economical to soak cabbage in brine than to use enough precious salt to dry-salt a juicy cabbage. Some researchers claim that cheap salt in the late medieval period and the Renaissance was the key factor that led to a population explosion in Baltic countries. Preserving

Lactobacillus isolated from sauerkraut.

cabbage (and herring) gave peasants enough nutrition to survive in regions with poor soil and short growing seasons.

The *Qimin Yaoshu* makes it sound like cabbage was not terribly important in China. It is mentioned in passing in an article about turnips, and given far fewer column inches than that giant of Chinese cuisine, the mallow (*Malva sylvestris*). After the tenth century, their positions reversed, with cabbage ascendant, as a vegetable astrologer might say. One theory is that the perennial mallow – yes, the plant that gave us the name 'marshmallow' for sticky sugar fluff – was valued because there were no sources of vegetable oil, and the mallow's mucilaginous leaves would thicken and mellow sauces and stews. Once technology for pressing oils became available, no one bothered to eat gummy leaves any more, and Chinese cabbage and its annual-growing kin were preferred for their robust growth and tender leaves.

Pickles made of cabbage were being packed by the third century BCE in the West, but they were preserved by soaking in sour wine, vinegar or verjuice with salt. Medieval pickled cabbage was packed in so much salt it had to be rinsed before it could be eaten. Sauerkraut, by contrast, is fermented. That means that it is preserved by the good graces of bacteria – *Leuconostoc mesenteroides* at first, when the cabbage is still fairly raw and alkaline, then *Lactobacillus brevis I* and *Lactobacillus plantarum* as the juices become more acidic. Sauerkraut-makers chop their cabbage into fine bits, mix it evenly with salt, then press the mixture down in a crock or jar, cover the mass and weigh it down. The fermenting sauerkraut generally contains between 1.5 and 4 per cent salt by weight – enough to draw out the cabbage juices without poisoning too many of the useful microbes. The weight ensures that the salty cabbage will stay submerged, a necessary step. The charming creatures that ferment cabbage into near-immortality only thrive when cabbage is held completely under liquid. If these creatures of the hidden kingdom are exposed them to air, they die, leaving cabbage open to moulds and various slimy, stinking microbes.

Crock pot for home-made sauerkraut.

Pushcart advertising 'frankfurts' with sauerkraut or onions for 5 cents, New York, c. 1939.

The bacteria devour sugars in the cabbage juice, excreting acids as they go. Happily, acidic liquid preserves much of the original cabbage's vitamin C. A properly fermented sauerkraut has a distinctive sharp smell and a sharp to acid taste, but none of the stench of cabbage left out in the open air to rot. The glucosinolates and other sulphur compounds that give cooking (or rotting) cabbages their putrid aroma are completely broken down by fermentation, never to return. If your home-made sauerkraut has an air of sewer-gas, it has been invaded by aerobic bacteria, and there is no cure. Throw it out!

Commercial sauerkraut fermentation tanks can hold up to 100 tons or more of shredded or chopped cabbage. Industrial producers remove the core of the cabbage because it contains sucrose, which indirectly encourages the growth of *L. mesenteroides*, a decadent little bacteria that can make kraut slimy or stringy, although it is hard to understand how something could be both at once. The cabbage is dry-salted to produce brine with a salt concentration of 2–3 per cent by mass and hurled into one of those gargantuan tanks to be digested by well-controlled bacteria. (Although at least one scientific food researcher claims that you don't need to bother with seeding bacteria if you start with 2 per cent salt and keep the kraut-to-be at 18°C/64°F.) European manufacturers package their wares about a week after fermentation begins, when a delicate piquancy develops; Americans, ever the devotees of venerable foods, sometimes leave their sauerkraut in tanks for up to a year before packing it off, creating impressively sour stuff.

Modern industrial sauerkraut is pasteurized before it is sold, killing all the helpful microbes that brought the cabbage so far. This state of affairs is unfortunate because there is increasing evidence – not baseless assertions by ascetics who eschew bathing, but actual scientific evidence – that the microbes we eat can transform the workings of human intestines, which, like sauerkraut crocks, are closed, liquid environments full of anaerobic bacteria.

Although sauerkraut seems like it has been part of German culture since the stuffing of the first *Blutwurst*, the first written description of sauerkraut occurs in a French – French! – volume titled *Le Trésor de santé* (1607), which describes it as 'German'. That version involves juniper, barberries and pepper, three exciting elements usually eliminated from modern banal sauerkrauts, which often simply taste of slightly sour cabbage and salt.

Once the sauerkraut has matured to perfect piquancy, there comes a time of decision: what do you do with all this sour cabbage? A confection called 'chocolate sauerkraut cake' or 'kraut fudge cake' has been creeping into American community cookbooks since the early 1970s. Various authors claim that it was a 1960s April Fool's joke, or the result of a USDA surplus food department contest for using kraut, or from a grandmother who travelled the Oregon Trail, or – more likely – a recipe from a pamphlet distributed by a sauerkraut company. The sauerkraut serves the same function as courgette or zucchini, or pumpkin in sweetened breads; it adds bulk and moisture without an overwhelming flavour (at least, it isn't overwhelming if you use chocolate). Received opinion about this cake is divergent; some diners swoon, others complain about finding cabbage threads in something they thought was cake. Although the pairing may seem bizarre, chocolate and sauerkraut do share flavour molecules in common, and the pairing intrigues some molecular gastronomers.

Kimchi

Although the microbes that produce kimchi are similar to sauerkraut's, the techniques for making it are substantially different. Cabbage (*baechu*) kimchi starts with whole cabbages cut in half lengthwise and soaked in brine that is 5–10 per cent salt, wilting the cabbage. After being washed and drained, the cabbage is packed into jars with prodigious amounts of red pepper, and smaller quantities of various other things – garlic, ginger, salted anchovy paste, green onions – for a final salt concentration of 3–6 per cent. The vegetables were traditionally packed in earthen jars and buried in the soil for a relatively steady year-round temperature. The same bacteria show up at roughly the same time as in sauerkraut: lactic acid bacteria munch first, but are superseded by more acid-tolerant organisms as the fermentation progresses. However, kimchi is fermented for a shorter time than traditional sauerkraut. Modern kimchi fanciers use a special kimchi refrigerator in their homes that keep the ferment at 18°C for a few days, then keep it at not-quite-freezing temperatures for as long as its maker can stand to wait. The procedure allows the kimchi to get a little sour, but not so much that the poor *Lactobacillus* bacteria acidify themselves out of existence. The ideal kimchi is a salty, spicy mixture that is slightly sour, without mature sauerkraut's sinus-clearing acid jolts. (It seems curious that the Germans would be as enthusiastic about salt-based fermentation as the Koreans, who live on a peninsula surrounded by brine.)

As with all cabbage dishes, there are regional variations. According to one modern Korean author,

> Northern regions tend to make bland and light kimchi to maintain the freshness of cabbage [to suit] their shorter summer and long winter . . . the southern region

A bowl of kimchi.

has higher temperatures, and they make salty and spicy kimchi to keep it from going sour or bad.

Until the mid-twentieth century, villagers serving kimchi to guests followed a kimchi hierarchy. One oral history recounts how poor villagers would eat 'coarse kimchi', made with the outer cabbage leaves and mere streaks of red pepper, served straight out of the jar. In contrast to this wan, soft, sloppy kimchi, honoured guests and elders were served plump, crunchy centre-leaf kimchi, scarlet with pepper and neatly arranged in a bowl.

There are claims, based on excavations of stoneware crocks, that Koreans have been preserving vegetables in salt for at least 5,000 years, but these artefacts may have simply been used for storing food packed in salt. The most famous of modern kimchi's main ingredients – cabbage and hot peppers – only appear in Korean records starting in the seventeenth

Kimchi jars at a South Korean home.

century during the Joseon dynasty. Exactly when Koreans started using napa cabbage for kimchi is hotly disputed by Korean researchers. Quotes such as 'I want to tear a person limb from limb like the way we tear kimchi' (Kungye of Hubaekje, 857?–918) imply that something was being torn – but that could have been scallions, or mallow, or mustard greens, or some other vegetable altogether. Probably the first reference to salted cabbage in Korea is from the poet Yi Kyu-bo, who wrote, 'radish pickled in soy sauce is good for three months in summer, salted cabbage for nine months of winter,' which is also one of the most pessimistic descriptions of Korea's climate ever to be published.

The *Hyangyak gugubbang* (Folk Medicine Emergency Remedies, 1236–51), the oldest surviving Korean medical text, states that 'cabbage has a sweet gentle taste to it and is without poison.' It also mentions that Seoul cabbage-growers had the same problem with hybrid cabbages as the poor Alexandrians – that if they saved seeds from their crops for three years, their cabbages would turn into turnips, that is, revert to a wild cabbage. Koreans were forced to buy their cabbage seeds from Beijing.

However, guides to kimchi-making up through the seventeenth century barely mention cabbage; turnips, radishes, cucumber, aubergine or eggplant, onions, chives and several other vegetables are far more popular. The first known mention of cabbage kimchi (as opposed to any other kind of kimchi) didn't occur until the *Sallim gyeongje* was published in 1766, where it is listed along with forty other types of kimchi – including kimchis made of bulrush or cattails (*hyang-po*).

Cabbage was very expensive and highly prized when it was first introduced to Korea. In the early fifteenth century, in the first years of the Joseon dynasty, villagers from Gyeonggi province were asked to bring cabbages to the shrine devoted to King Sejong's mother every day in April and May. At first, cabbage was chiefly grown just outside the gates of Hanyang (now Seoul). As the royal court expanded, so did cabbage farming, reaching the Seoul suburbs, but it was apparently primarily consumed by the wealthy, and there are records of cabbage seeds still being imported from China until at least 1533. Cabbage kimchi with pepper and fish sauce started getting popular in the eighteenth century. Cabbage cultivation spread through Korea, and cabbage started inching towards the top of official vegetable lists. Chilli peppers arrived in Korea around the time of the Imjin wars in 1592, and were rapidly incorporated into kimchi-making. By the early nineteenth century the scholar Jeong Yak-yong wrote in his *Gyeongse yupyo* (Design for Good Government) that 'Inside and outside Seoul and in big cities, people made several tens of thousands of *jeon* from selling green onion, garlic cabbage, cucumber from 10 *myo* (about 1 acre) of dry fields.' It is not clear how much one *jeon* of currency was worth in 1820s Korea, much less tens of thousands, but Jeong himself planted cabbage in half of his house's garden. By 1907 cabbage was being grown in Hamgyong, Korea's northernmost province, and the price had come down to modern levels of circa U.S.$1.5–$3 a head in today's money. Various other kimchi ingredients – fish sauce, hot peppers – underwent similar transformations from prized luxuries to everyday Korean grub.

During the Japanese occupation of Korea in the early twentieth century, thousands of Koreans picked up and moved to the cities – creating a new governmental headache during *kimjang* season, when family and neighbours gather to make the year's kimchi. Tons of cabbage, radishes, peppers and other seasonings had to be transported to the cities for special *kimjang* markets for three weeks every autumn. These markets also generated tons of waste, mostly discarded outer cabbage

Salted Chinese cabbage for kimchi.

leaves, and contemporary newspapers reported on the piles of rubbish piling up in Incheon, Yongsan and other cities – a problem that continued well into the 1960s. *Kimjang* was also hampered by water shortages and restricted supplies in many cities that had built new waterworks in the 1920s and '30s, causing considerable kimchi consternation.

In pre-industrial Korea, the traditional time for *kimjang* was 7 November – late enough in the season that the kimchi wouldn't sour too quickly, but early enough that vegetables hadn't been damaged by frost. In the 1950s, *kimjang* timing has shifted to 25 November – the day of the month when many Korean workers are paid, and can afford to buy massive quantities of cabbage. Some companies paid a *kimjang* bonus in November to help their kimchi-craving employees. Today, Koreans pay for cabbage with credit cards, and *kimjangs* take place on weekends, when families get time off from school and work.

Kimjang: kimchi making for the winter.

Kimchi's hot peppers set it apart from Chinese *yancai* and Japanese pickled vegetables, and its smell is distinctive, to put it politely. As the Korean researcher Cho Hong Sik wrote, 'Up until the early sixties, kimchi was an embarrassment in the intercultural settings. Koreans admitted that kimchi smells awful. Although Koreans could not stop eating kimchi, they dared not publicly urge foreigners to learn to enjoy kimchi.' In the 1970s, Korean 'guest workers' labouring on construction in the Middle East spurred a market for kimchi exports, but most researchers pin kimchi's stardom on the 1988 Seoul Olympics. After two decades of rapid industrialization, urbanization and living under a military dictatorship, when more and more women bought kimchi at supermarkets on their way home from work, Koreans latched onto a homely food evoking villages of cackling mothers-in-law stuffing cabbage into stone crocks. At a time when cabbage is gradually disappearing from Western menus, Korea is staunchly defending its cabbagey kimchi as a cultural icon.

The first kimchi museum was established in 1986 in a Seoul food factory, but it was bought and moved to the Seoul Olympic site in 1988. Kimchi became part of the official menu for the Seoul games, and for all Korean athletes since, inspiring cryptic announcements like 'Korean football is the force of kimchi' (2002 Football World Cup).

Kimchi is alleged to prevent cancer, constipation, high blood pressure, diabetes, even avian flu. In 1996 the Ministry of Culture and Sports proclaimed kimchi and *bulgogi* barbecue, eaten together, as one of the top five Korean cultural symbols, along with the Korean alphabet, traditional dress and tae kwon do, and the Bulgug Buddhist Temple.

In the 1990s South Korea entered into an international trade dispute with Japan over kimchi. Japanese manufacturers had begun to produce a food they called *kimuchi*, a Japanese version of the venerable Korean cabbage that Koreans saw as a derangement of their national dish, and had the temerity to suggest that *kimuchi* be one of the official Japanese foods at the 1996 Atlanta Olympics. Korean kimchi manufacturers cried foul, and filed a case with the Codex Alimentarius, the standards body of the Food and Agriculture Organization of the United

The 2014 Seoul Kimchi Making and Sharing Festival.

Nations. Some Japanese producers skipped the fermentation and added artificial sour flavouring using citric acid and gum. 'What the Japanese are selling is nothing more than cabbage sprinkled with seasonings and artificial flavourings,' said Robert Kim, an assistant manager at Doosan, South Korea's largest kimchi producer. In 2001 the Codex Alimentarius published a voluntary standard defining kimchi as 'a fermented food that uses salted napa cabbages as its main ingredient mixed with seasonings, and goes through a lactic acid production process at a low temperature.' The Codex was mum on how long kimchi had to be fermented – ten seconds? Two weeks? – and on what additives were forbidden.

In 2000 South Koreans produced 1.5 million tons of kimchi – 450,000 tons in kimchi factories, and more than a million tons at home. By 2005 Chinese kimchi makers were creeping into the market, exporting 100,000 tons of kimchi to Korea each year, and the 'kimchi wars' began. In 2005 Korean politicians

Korean-American supermarket kimchi jar display.

falsely charged that Chinese kimchi contained lead, and the Korean Food and Drug Administration found that some Chinese-made kimchi contained parasite eggs – presumably from cabbage-pickers with poor hygiene habits. In retaliation, Chinese inspectors declared some Korean kimchi contained parasite eggs, too, and banned its import. That particular skirmish ended with a mutual agreement for more inspections. China also decided that fermented kimchi from Korea bore too high a risk of hoarding coliform bacteria, and in 2010 barred imported Korean kimchi that had not been pasteurized. Imports resumed in 2016.

A poor Korean cabbage harvest in 2010 left thousands of Koreans wringing their hands, if not their cabbage, and the Seoul city government even instituted a kimchi bailout programme to subsidize the price of 300,000 heads of cabbage it had purchased to supply urban demand.

In 2011, at South Korea's request, UNESCO included *kimjang*, 'making and sharing kimchi in the Republic of Korea,' on the Representative List of the Intangible Cultural Heritage of Humanity, affirming:

> The collective practice of Kimjang reaffirms Korean identity and is an excellent opportunity for strengthening family cooperation. Kimjang is also an important reminder for many Koreans that human communities need to live in harmony with nature. Preparation follows a yearly cycle . . . There are regional differences, and the specific methods and ingredients used in Kimjang are considered an important family heritage, typically transmitted from a mother-in-law to her newly married daughter-in-law.

4
The Food of the People
(and Their Cows)

Poor Mr. Bucket, however hard he worked . . . was never able
make enough to buy one-half of the things that so large a family
needed. There wasn't even enough money to buy proper food
for them all. The only meals they could afford were bread and
margarine for breakfast, boiled potatoes and cabbage for lunch,
and cabbage soup for supper.

Roald Dahl, *Charlie and the Chocolate Factory* (1964)

Despite its popularity, for centuries cabbage's culinary destiny
has been shaped by its status as the food of the poor – or,
in times of plenty, as fodder for cattle and horses. A friend
described by M.F.K. Fisher summarized the matter when she
smelled boiled cabbage, blurting out 'Oh! We're in the slums!'
Although cabbage is celebrated in the world of food photog-
raphy, thanks to its astonishing structure, it continues to be
neglected in haute cuisine and modernist menus.

Cabbage took a lowly role in the medieval concept of the
Great Chain of Being, in which edible creatures of the sky
(songbirds, geese) were considered far superior to anything
that came from water (fish) or from the ground (vegetables).
Cabbage did not have the distinction of occupying the abso-
lute lowest rung of edible matter – that was reserved for earthy

vegetables such as turnips and onions – but cabbage wasn't far off.

At one time, cabbage was fit for a king. Cabbages appear on a list of seeds bought for King John's English household in 1360 when he was confined to castle arrest. Inventories of Charlemagne's estates in ninth-century France list very few vegetables as being grown in royal gardens, but cabbages do make the list, along with celery, turnips, kohlrabi, beetroot, and leeks, garlic, shallots and onions – the makings of a nutritious, monotonous diet, or perhaps a banquet for the King of the Onions. Some authors claim that Charlemagne wouldn't even let his staff eat the brassica kohlrabi, for fear it would make men 'soft': instead, it was fed to horses. This notion is strange because Charlemagne's *Capitulare de villis*, or *On the Management of Estates*, exhorts his subjects to plant a wide variety of vegetables including cucumbers, pumpkins, kidney beans, chickpeas, lettuces, rocket salad, garden cress, celery, beetroot, carrots,

Joachim Beuckelaer, *The Four Elements: Earth. A Fruit and Vegetable Market with the Flight into Egypt in the Background*, 1569, oil on canvas.

parsnips, orach, spinach, kohlrabi, cabbages, onions, chives, leeks, radishes, shallots, garlic, broad beans, peas and 'house-leeks'. It could be that most of these vegetables were not particularly long-lasting, and only eaten in season and not stored, and did not figure into estate-keepers' accounting. Accounting methods had a profound effect on cabbage's popularity. In the late Middle Ages, cabbages moved from being grown in odd areas between fields to kitchen gardens next to peasants' homes. Tenants paid no taxes to their landlord for produce from these plots, making them extremely attractive places to grow edibles.

Untaxable food was important simply because peasants did not have much money to spend. In 1457 a survey of King René's properties in Provence found that peasants spent 86 per cent of their food budget on grains for pottage or bread

Pieter de Hooch, *A Woman with a Duck and a Woman with a Cabbage*, *c.* 1677–84, oil on canvas.

and wine, while wealthier overseers only spent 60 per cer̲
of their monies on grains and cheering beverages. Cheeses,
hams, brandy, cabbage – everything that was not bread or wine
came from a limited pool of money for most peasants. The
same was true for British peasants of the time period, who
also spent most of their money on grains.

The historian Louis Stouff, challenging the pleasant
tourist-office tableau of Provençal peasants revelling in pud-
dles of tapenade and aioli, documented in his history of
fourteenth- to fifteenth-century Provençal food supplies that
the overwhelming proportion of the ordinary Provençal
residents' food supply consisted of salt pork, peas, beans and
cabbage – much like the rest of Europe at the time. 'Traditional'
Provençal cooking appears to date to the nineteenth century,
when cabbages began to fall out of fashion (again).

A song by Neidhart von Reuental, a famous Bavarian
Minnesinger poet of the thirteenth century, describes cabbages
as punishment. A young cad is punished for his depredations
on local women when he marries a strict wife who does not
indulge his taste for luxury. Reuental says, roughly, 'He'll be
eating all kinds of cabbages forever. It'll make his hair stand
on end.'

Whatever the cause, this mental state of vegetal poverty
persisted in northern Europe and France – France! – for
centuries. *Le Viandier de Taillevent*, the influential cookbook
published at the end of the fifteenth century, only mentions
five vegetables: cabbage, peas, fava or broad beans, leeks and
onions. Taillevent had roughly the same variety of vegetables
in his diet as a fussy four-year-old. As the historian Victoria
Dickenson notes,

> From 1300 to 1660, the percentage of dishes including
> vegetables quadrupled, while the number of species

mentioned in cookbooks doubled . . . By the mid-seventeenth century Nicolas de Bonnefons included fifty-six pages of recipes for vegetables, including such new foods as pumpkin (citrouille), potatoes, and haricot beans in *Les délices de la campagne.*

The seventeenth century saw transformations in European food culture. A new generation of French royal chefs took it upon themselves to denounce the spice- and stuffing-heavy cuisine of medieval and Renaissance kitchens. Nicolas de Bonnefons, valet in the court of Louis XIV, naturally turned to the cabbage as a symbol of authenticity, writing 'let the cabbage soup taste entirely of cabbage . . . leaving elaborate mixtures of chopped meat, diced vegetables, breadcrumbs and other deceptions for the kinds of dishes which are for simply tasting rather than filling oneself up on.'

Even in 1803, Grimod de La Reynière, in his *Almanach des gourmands*, felt the need to write as a cabbage apologist:

> Cabbage is a great help in cooking, even in sophisticated cooking. A talented artist knows how to derive an advantageous result from this vegetable, unjustly scorned by the arrogant, to vary his soups, garnishes, and side dishes . . . Just as the most vulgar terms are ennobled under the pen of a great poet, a cabbage *à la bavaroise*, which by that name is the preferred bed of an andouille sausage, is no ordinary stew.

Grimod also praises sauerkraut as 'shedding the cabbage of all its negative qualities'.

Monsieur de La Reynière may have been partly reacting to the spread of cabbage as a fodder crop across the Channel. Some classicists have posited that the word 'brassica' is a

Pieter Aertsen, *Market Woman at a Vegetable Stand*, 1567, oil on wood.

contraction of *praesecare* (to cut off early), implying that farmers cut leaves off their cabbages to feed their animals. Although Dutch farmers had used cabbages as a winter fodder crop since the late Middle Ages, news of the cabbage's suitability for supporting cows and sheep seems to have made its way to Britain in the late seventeenth century, and was rediscovered in the eighteenth century after various crop failures made grain a scarce commodity for livestock. As historian Robert Trow-Smith explains, 'It had the virtue, which turnips had not, of surviving a hard winter, standing for early spring feeding . . . cows yielded half-a-gallon more milk a day upon it than on any other winter food.' Since those milky times, the turnip

James Peale, *Still-life: Balsam Apples and Vegetables*, *c.* 1820s, oil on canvas.

and swede – yet another brassica cross-breed, this time between *Brassica oleracea* and *Brassica rapa* – have overtaken cabbage as a fodder and forage crop for livestock.

Cabbage's accounting had become more standardized in Britain as well. No longer a charming relic of kitchen gardens, cabbage was now a full-fledged field crop, as Adam Smith observed in 1776:

> Potatoes . . . cost half the price which they used to do thirty or forty years ago. The same thing may be said of turnips, carrots, cabbages; things which were formerly never raised but by the spade, but which are now commonly raised by the plough.

By then, cabbage was established throughout the New World. Jacques Cartier's Canadian settlements started growing cabbages in 1540, and cabbages, kale and collards were

grown in western Hispaniola (Haiti) by 1565. North America
Massachusetts Bay Colony got into the act by 1631, when
governor John Winthrop ordered seeds from a London grocer
including 1 ounce of colewort (collard) seeds, 8 ounces of
'cabedge' seeds, and 2 ounces of 'culiflower' seeds. The only
other seeds Winthrop ordered by the half-pound was radishes.
Colonists in Virginia are recorded as growing cabbages by 1669.
Broccoli and Brussels sprouts seem to have arrived in the New
World in the eighteenth and nineteenth centuries respectively.
German colonists toted sauerkraut traditions with them wher-
ever they went – to Lunenburg, Nova Scotia, in 1753, when
Germans and Swiss were recruited by General Cornwallis to
supplement (or perhaps supplant) the English population.
Cabbages didn't just appeal to homesick Europeans. Bernard
Romans, a map-maker who travelled to what is now Missis-
sippi in the late 1770s, observed that the Choctaw people were
farming cabbages, leeks, garlic, hogs and ducks – although he
claimed all this agriculture was only for trade. However, there

Cabbage at Wynne Farm, a mountaintop training facility for farmers in
Kenscoff, Haiti.

Arthur Melville, *A Cabbage Garden*, 1877, oil on canvas.

is a strong oral tradition that the Choctaw ate plenty of he
meat; it isn't much of a stretch to imagine that they enjoyed
the other foods they produced as well.

Through the nineteenth century, cabbage continued to
be a food of last resort among poor European peasants in
northern countries. A visitor to Russia's Ryazan province,
some 200 km (124 mi.) southeast of Moscow, commented,
'Vegetables are not eaten much as the peasants do not have
good vegetable gardens . . . only cabbage is used much and
also onions and radishes on fast days. The peasants hardly
know any other vegetables.'

By the middle of the nineteenth century, cheap, easy-to-
cook cabbage was the only vegetable many American families
ever ate. In an 1874 survey of the diets of Massachusetts work-
ing-class families, 40 per cent reported that they didn't eat any
vegetables other than cabbage and potatoes on a daily basis,
and another 55 per cent ate vegetables other than cabbage and
potatoes only once a day. Today's Americans follow a similar
plan, but they have dispensed with the cabbage: today tomatoes and potatoes make up more than half of total vegetable
consumption across all age groups.

This pattern persisted among low-income groups in the
u.s. despite improved transportation and refrigeration – likely
because poorer Americans didn't have access to either. A 1936
survey of African Americans showed that in one week the
average family's weekly vegetable consumption consisted of
450 g (1 lb) of tomatoes (fresh or tinned), 540 g (1.2 lb) of
cabbage or other greens, and 590 g (1.3 lb) of green beans.

In the southern United States, the status of collard greens
and cabbage is problematic because these brassicas historically
have not just been the food of the poor, but the food of
slaves. As one author put it, 'Are foods such as pig's feet,
collard greens, black-eyed peas, and hominy grits simply

)uthern home cooking," or should they be identified as the
.ood of slaves?' Plenty of Southern families cook collard
greens and cabbage today, but collard greens or cabbage slowly
braised with pork – particularly pork fat or fatback – is one
of the signature dishes of soul food, the traditional cuisine
of descendants of African American slaves.

In the 1960s Elijah Muhammad, the African American
cleric who led the Nation of Islam, a predominantly African
American denomination, warned:

> Peas, collard greens, turnip greens, sweet potatoes and
> white potatoes are very cheaply raised foods. The South-
> ern slave masters used them to feed the slaves, and still
> advise the consumption of them. Most white people of

Corned beef and cabbage, as served on St Patrick's Day at the Canadian
Honker Restaurant in Rochester, Minnesota.

the middle and upper class do not eat this lot of cheap food, which is unfit for human consumption.

Muhammad also advised against eating green cabbage leaves and 'cabbage sprouts'; the white interior leaves of cabbages were acceptable. By avoiding 'slave foods', Muhammad's followers could clean their minds of slaveholders' ideology, and stop accepting their degradation, feeding themselves food only fit for animal fodder. In succeeding decades, following Elijah Muhammad's death in 1975, Nation of Islam members have reclaimed collards and other soul food, seeing the food as a source of African American pride. These cooks are choosing to follow traditional Sunni Islamic rules on halal and haram foods – pork is still not allowed – instead of Muhammad's strictures based on slaves' lives.

In 2016 the Neiman Marcus department store highlighted this contradiction by selling a 1.3-kg (3-lb) batch of prepared collard greens for $66 (plus $15.50 shipping) at a time when collard greens cost roughly $0.86 per lb at a grocery store. This traditional African American soul food made with a cabbage relative widely thought to have been brought to the U.S. by slaves, and commonly prepared by Southern slaves and their descendants, was simply advertised as being 'seasoned with just the right amount of spices and bacon', with no reference to the black cooks who originated the dish and prepared it for generations. A food of the poor was gentrified, and the poor people who originated it were erased from the story, as the *Washington Post*'s Janelle Fox observed.

By contrast, Irish Americans demand corned beef and cabbage to celebrate St Patrick's Day (17 March) – a practice that confounds people actually living in Ireland. The dish is unknown in the mother country, although bacon and cabbage is common. Corned beef was likely substituted by Irish American immigrants because it was a luxury good in nineteenth-century Ireland, and generally only eaten on occasions like Easter and Christmas. In America, corned beef was cheap enough that every day could be a holiday. The meal of cabbage is elevated to sacred status by its companion meat; Irish Americans do not take pride in stewing turkey sausage with cabbage.

In modern times, cabbage's mundane nature made a perfect subject for the 'Cabbage Memo' – or 'The Great Cabbage Hoax', as American folklorists termed it. Before the Second World War, the United States imported 90 per cent of its supply of cabbage seeds from out of the country – just as residents of Alexandria and Korea (but not Italy) had done centuries before. Unfortunately, the u.s. was importing seeds from the Netherlands, and when the Nazis blockaded the North Atlantic, the only seed growers in the u.s. were Dutch farmers living near Puget Sound. A California businessman bought up the entire crop for $1.75 per lb, then turned around and started charging other farmers $17 per lb for cabbage seed.

The Office of Price Administration (OPA) – a wartime office specifically created to stop this kind of price gouging – stepped in and wrote a directive setting a price ceiling on cabbage seed on 19 August 1943. OPA regulations demanded that all terms be defined, and the directive included the statement '"cabbage seed" (*Brassica capitata*) is the seed used to grow cabbage.' Shortly afterwards, the OPA got a telegram from the Kansas City Mercantile Exchange, stating:

> The Ten Commandments contain 297 words
> The Lord's Prayer 56
> The Declaration of Independence 1,821
> The Gettysburg Address 266
> And it took an OPA lawyer 2,611 words to say cabbage seed (*Brassica capitata*) is the seed used to grow cabbage.

School children holding one of the large heads of cabbage raised in the war garden of Public School 88, Queens, New York City, *c.* 1918.

In point of fact, the entire regulation is closer to 2,200 words, and also deals with issues such as how the maximum price of cabbage seed is determined – information that would deeply concern seed salesmen in the Kansas City Mercantile Exchange. But the die was cast, and for the past seventy years this particular formulation has been used repeatedly by government-loathing commentators – usually substituting

phrase 'The U.S. government regulations on the sale of
ɔage: 26,911 words' for the comments about the OPA
'er.

Such price control ended in December 1943, but the
ɔage-regulation canard has persisted, zombie-like, despite
ated attempts to debunk it. Senator Orrin Hatch – ever
to over-regulation – recited the bogus cabbage statistics
ɔ95, whereupon they were entered into the Congressional
Record, and an episode of the popular television show *The West
Wing* in 2002 highlighted the imaginary cabbage data.

The Cabbage Memo only succeeds because it concerns
cabbages – a lowly, common food, not worthy of anyone's
attention. No one would question a 2,611-word regulation on
the sale of diamonds, or champagne, or industrial oil-drilling
equipment. But cabbage is a simple thing . . . until an avaricious
businessman threatens the nation's entire supply.

5
Our Cabbage,
Right or Wrong

Whatever you do, make it Polish. Put cabbage in.
Anonymous woman's advice to Chicago settlement house
workers, as reported by the home economist and author
Florence Nesbitt

Pittsburgh, for some reason I have never understood,
had a passion for cabbages; and why Pittsburgh hasn't
produced more so-called realistic writers, in the
Russian manner, I cannot understand.
Sherwood Anderson, *A Story-teller's Story* (1924)

Cabbage has a charisma that turnips can only dream of, and
many ethnic groups share strong affection for cabbage dishes.
Can you be Polish and not eat *gołąbki* (cabbage rolls)? Shchi,
kapuśniak, *garbure*, *Rotkohl*, kimchi, colcannon, corned beef and
cabbage – cabbage-based foods evoke the humble home, even
if their origins are questionable and their preparations have
become more stylish and fanciful over the centuries. Corned
beef and cabbage most likely originated in New York bars,
not Ireland, but it remains a symbol of Irish Americans' link
to home even though the dish is also served in Newfoundland
under the name 'Jiggs Dinner', and has no special cachet.

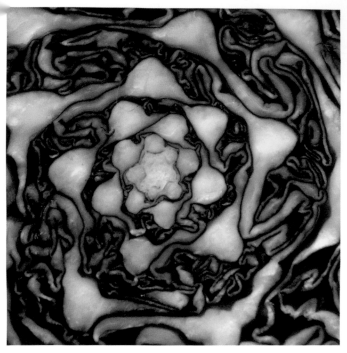
Red cabbage interior.

Modern Polish *gołąbki* are made with rice, a food that is not now, and has never been, grown in Poland.

Cabbage and sauerkraut dishes acquire new titles at an astonishing rate. The named dishes are generally made with meat, and are served at celebrations and weddings, but they tend to be variations on common foods. It almost seems as if cabbage subtly sabotages regional culinary creativity, reducing cooks to merely redecorating the same basic foods over and over again. Three types of cabbage dishes in particular are claimed as national treasures by at least a dozen nations: cabbage soup, cabbage rolls and sauerkraut cooked with meat.

Cabbage Soup

The word 'soup' in English comes from *suppa* in Frankish, which comes from Danish *sopen*, to sop or soak in English. All this sopping refers to the European tradition from medieval times onward of putting bread in a bowl and pouring soup over it. The classic French cabbage soup *garbure* is one of these bread-sopping soups, as is the cabbage soup featured in the 1981 French comedy film *La Soupe aux choux* (Cabbage Soup), about an extraterrestrial alien who becomes enamoured of a couple of old French farmers' cabbage soup – much as Zeus and Hermes were charmed by Philemon and Baucis's cabbage with salt pork.

But in France, there is cabbage soup, and there is cabbage soup. In *Les Bons plats de France*, published in 1913, Pampille, also known as Marthe Allard Daudet, included cabbage soup as one of her four 'most important national soups of France', soups that were eaten by the rich and poor in every region. However, the exact contents of that soup were very different for the rich and poor. Mme Marceline Michaux's 1867 cookbook *La Cuisine de la ferme* (In the Farm Kitchen) was published with approval from the French Ministry of Agriculture to improve peasant cooking. Mme Michaux had a low opinion of peasant cooking, writing that they had 'a primitive, traditional diet, always the same or very nearly so for generations, sometimes insipid, sometimes overspiced . . . often costing more than if the food were more varied, flavoursome, and good.' Michaux's recipe for cabbage soup consisted of a cabbage boiled with a leek and a clove of garlic, with a little butter added at the end. By contrast, Alexandre Viard's *Le Cuisinier impérial*, a culinary encyclopedia that was published in at least 32 editions between 1805 and 1875, features a cabbage soup designed for a household with considerable leisure time.

nstead of simply boiling vegetables, Viard's cook is compelled to boil two whole cabbages, dry them out (!), then cook them with veal, bacon fat, carrots, onions and mushrooms. *The Modern Housewife, or Ménagère* (1851), published in Britain for middle-class housewives by Alexis Soyer, suggests a 'French Cabbage Soup' with a happy medium of 2 lb (950 g) of streaky bacon boiled with the same weight of cabbage, two large onions, a carrot, a turnip and a head of celery, seasoned with a bit of brown sugar, pepper and salt. Soyer suggests serving the soup poured over a pound of sliced bread in a tureen. The recipe was good enough to plagiarize: a 1917 volume of *American Cookery* (formerly the *Boston Cooking School Magazine*) features a nearly identical recipe with the quantities halved.

Garbure is the classic soup of southwest France, which at its essence consists of cabbage, bacon, lard or – if you're lucky enough to live in Gascony – salt-preserved goose. A seventeenth-century observer wrote of Gascon cuisine, 'a

French cabbage soup preparations.

little piece of this old salt goose can be added to cabbage to make a good, white, thick soup which is the common nourishment of the villagers and the poor.' Julia Child called her *garbure* a 'fine and uncomplicated peasant soup', although her version is fancied up with potatoes, peppercorns, parsley, marjoram, thyme, garlic, onions and carrots. Soups for festive occasions in southwest France include *garbure gersoise* and *garbure landaise*, which both contain copious amounts of duck, duck confit and duck fat in addition to bacon or ham.

The French immigrants who had the misfortune to land in the part of Atlantic Canada nicknamed Acadia – only to be expelled by the British in 1755 – brought over a meatless cabbage and turnip concoction called 'Soup à la Toussaint', traditionally eaten on All Saints' Day in France. Supposedly this was the Acadians' favourite soup at the time of the expulsion. Once the luckless Acadians made their way to Louisiana, they adopted filé gumbo soup instead, abandoning cabbage for the delights of okra.

Beyond France, there is Russia. 'Shchi and kasha are our food,' goes the Russian peasant saying, an homage to shchi, the cabbage soup which feeds the Russian soul. It is not clear where or when shchi emerged – Russian authors claim it dates back to the tenth century, but don't say how they know – but by 1877 a French traveller described shchi as 'a mixture of chopped cabbage, barley meal, and salt, together with a modicum of *kvass* (a beverage made of rye bread fermented in water)'. But like the Russian soul, shchi is not a single, constant thing. Joyce Toomre notes there are thirteen different recipes for shchi in Elena Molokhovets's classic nineteenth-century Russian-language cookbook *Gift to Young Housewives*, but the basic procedure for all of them is the same: make broth of beef, mushrooms or fish, add chopped greens and a thickener (barley or flour) and add condiments like sour cream, parsley

Cabbage field, Dojran region, Macedonia.

or dill just before serving. A rich man might have a beef broth and tender spring greens; a peasant, sauerkraut and *kvass*. The defining aspect of shchi is its sourness, not a particular green or acid ingredient – which may explain why it has never become particularly popular in non-Slavic kitchens. Today's shchis tend to add modern fripperies such as tinned tomatoes, beans, potatoes and marjoram – much like latter-day *garbure*. Is no one content with cabbage?

Ukrainians adapted shchi to their own purposes, removing the barley and adding beetroot (beets) to make borscht – which is also consumed throughout Russia and Eastern Europe. Ukrainians, Poles and dozens of other peoples also make *kapuśniak*, a soup of sauerkraut and pork sausage, often thickened with flour and containing any number of other ingredients – potatoes, carrots, tomato paste . . . Add sour cream, paprika, caraway seeds and a bit of stock to your sauerkraut soup and you have Hungarian *gulyás à la székely* or Czech *segedínský guláš* or even *zelňačka* sauerkraut soup, with or without mushrooms.

Portugal's beloved *caldo verde* soup is a potage of potatoes, onions, broth and yet another puzzling member of the brassica family: *Brassica oleracea* var. *costata*, also known as couve tronchuda, tronchuda kale, sea kale, Galician cabbage, braganza and a variety of other aliases. Tronchuda kale looks like a cross between collard greens and kale, with wide white veins in wide leaves and tender, fleshy stems that resemble tender broccoli or bok choy. It is praised as being sweeter and more tender than cabbage and other brassicas, and it is impossible to make proper *caldo verde* without it.

Spanish *caldo gallego*, or Galician soup, is a variant of *caldo verde* – a natural consequence of Galicia's perch to the north of Portugal. The Galicians add meat and white beans to their green soup for reasons known only to them, and substitute *grelos* – local turnip greens – for the couve tronchuda. *Cocido madrileño*, another of Spain's most famous soups, also features cabbage, but in a supporting role: the quantities of pork, sausage and chickpeas in the pot tend to outshine any vegetables.

Transporting vegetables in Gradce, Slovenia, 1956.

Black cabbage soup is enjoyed – where else? – near the Black Sea. Sautéed meat and onions are joined by corn, white beans, a little tomato purée and shredded cabbage for a soup not entirely unlike *caldo gallego.*

Not quite soup, and not quite solid, greens – including cabbage – cooked in meat stock are a central feature of the cuisine of the Southern United States, a cooking method that can be traced back to cooking by slaves taken from West Africa, where Portuguese and other European recipes merged with indigenous cuisines. Jean Barbot, a member of the Senegal company, reported from Guinea in the 1680s: 'The rich [Africans] often have the meat of pigs, goats, harts and cows . . . from which they even make cabbage soup, and several other stews which they have learned from the whites and passed on from one to another.'

Cabbage soup has been a feature of European prisons for centuries as well. Lt Paul Gambaiana, an American airman imprisoned in the Swiss Wauwilermoos internment camp in 1944 recalls that his crew

> wanted to get back to our base so we attempted to leave Switzerland, and they got us and put us there. It was a Swiss concentration camp. About the only thing I can remember . . . we had cabbage soup which was hot water and two leaves of cabbage floating . . .

Cabbage Rolls

The term *sarma* for cabbage rolls comes from the Turkish word *sarmak*, which means to wrap – as opposed to *dolma*, from *dolmak*, or 'to be stuffed'. Take a cabbage leaf and roll it around a handful of rice, and you have *sarma*; take a head of cabbage, cut out the centre, and put a scoop of rice in, and you have *dolma*.

Stuffed cabbage leaves span the distance from the Balkans to the Arctic Circle: from the *sarma* of the Balkans and the Middle East, to the Swedish stuffed cabbage *dolma*, named identically to the Turks' dish – supposedly because Sweden's King Charles xii brought it back from Turkey. Eastern European nations inexplicably name their cabbage rolls 'little doves', or 'little pigeons' if you live in the city. Polish *gołąbki*, Ukrainian *holubtsi*, Lithuanian *balendalai* and Russian *golubtsy* are all little birds – cabbage rolls filled with a mixture of meat and rice. Still another Russian variation where the cabbage is not rolled, but simply chopped up with meat and rice, is called *lenivye golubtsy*, or, for the literal-minded, 'lazy little pigeons'. There are endless variations; Russians serve theirs with a sweet-and-sour sauce and sour cream, the Ukrainians fill them with buckwheat, millet, cornflour (cornstarch) or occasionally even yeast dough (although that variation is generally wrapped in beet greens).

The ingredients change from north to south, east to west. Romanians, Serbians, Croatians and other Balkan residents use leaves of sauerkraut to wrap their meaty packages; in the Middle East, some *sarma* have no meat at all. Among the Jews who eat cabbage rolls on Simchat Torah, 'Many Hungarian Jews use a dash of marjoram, Syrians add cinnamon, Persians throw in some dill and mint, and Romanians toss in lots of garlic and paprika,' the *Jewish Telegraphic Agency* reports. They may be cooked in tomato sauce, broth or any other potable liquid around the house. There is also a tradition of wrapping bread dough in cabbage leaves before cooking it, as the people of Gascony, France, do with a millet bread called *brazaire*.

Stuffed cabbage – that is, an entire head of cabbage hollowed out and filled with something else – is another

Green cabbage in a supermarket.

pan-European dish. The filling usually contains chopped meat mixed with breadcrumbs or rice, egg, some chopped cabbage leaves, some member of the onion family (onions, garlic, leeks) and various flavourings – salt, pepper, whatever else is used in the region. As Allen S. Weiss, author of the essay *Autobiography in a Stuffed Cabbage*, writes,

This mixture is nearly invariable in the Rouergue, and it serves as a prime marker of national differences: while in France the filler is usually soaked bread, in Eastern Europe it will tend to be rice, as is the case in most versions in Hungary, where stuffed cabbage is tantamount to a national dish.

However, keeping a partly dissected head of cabbage whole through cooking is a difficult business, and, as Weiss observed, most nations make cabbage rolls instead – individual cabbage leaves wrapped around stuffing. Most Europeans make stuffed cabbage as a sour, salty dish. For example, Hungarians stew their stuffed cabbage in a sauce of cabbage, sauerkraut and tomato and top it with sour cream. However Polish residents living near Warsaw sometimes add raisins cooked in caramelized sugar, and many Eastern European Jewish recipes for stuffed cabbage and cabbage rolls add raisins, honey or crushed ginger-nut biscuits to the sauce.

Sauerkraut with Meat

Sausage or meat stewed in sauerkraut is a logical dish to try in any region with large supplies of sausage and sauerkraut. The Balkan *podvarak* is almost the same dish as Polish *bigos*; onions and sauerkraut are sautéed, then combined with meat and simmered and/or baked at low temperature in an oven and/or put in a slow cooker until tender. Substitute cabbage for the sauerkraut and stew it, and you have Serbian 'wedding cabbage'. Some versions of *podvarak* leave the meats in large pieces to brown as they bake; others are chopped small, as in *bigos*. The spices vary: Balkan cooks use garlic and hot peppers; Poles use calmer northern spices like marjoram and caraway

Polish *bigos* (sauerkraut stew).

seeds, and sweeteners such as honey and prunes, and chop everything small enough that *bigos* is often eaten as a chopped spread on rye toast as appetizer, not as a main course. It is also familiar to French cooks who cook *choucroute Alsacienne garnie* with sausages stewed in sauerkraut and wine.

There are also hints that *bigos* is derived from a sixteenth-century dish called *mizkudancja*, from the Italian *mescolanza*, meaning 'mixture' – of layers of meat, sauerkraut and onions. A similar dish persists among the Pennsylvania Dutch called gumbis, or, rarely, *knabrus*, which consists of layers of meat and shredded cabbage.

The curious thing about *bigos* is that, like British bubble and squeak, it did not originally contain any cabbage at all. In the seventeenth century, *bigos* was any of a variety of chopped dishes made of roasted meat, fish, capon, game, grouse, crayfish, bone marrow – almost anything but vegetables. However, all these savoury collations were soured with materials that were a bit too rich for the everyday Pole: lemon, lime, wine vinegar or sorrel. Substituting cabbage for some of the meat reduced the cost of meat and wine vinegar, making *bigos* cheaper all-around. 'Rascal bigos' – with cabbage corrupting the meat – started appearing in the eighteenth century, and proved practical enough that they became the default *bigos* recipe by the nineteenth century.

Of course, Germans make a version of this dish, because Germans are supposed to eat sauerkraut.

Dumplings

Half-moon-shaped dumplings made of circles of wheat dough folded and pleated around a filling travelled with the Mongol empire, spreading south to China and west to the Middle East, Russia, Poland and Ukraine. Although these adaptable culinary cases have been adapted to a variety of fillings, there is a strong penchant for wrapping cabbage in dough in the northern latitudes. Napa cabbage is a typical ingredient in northern Chinese *jiaozi* dumplings, along with pork, something from the onion tribe and soy sauce. To the west, *jiaozi* becomes Ukrainian *varynyky* or Polish *pierogi*, which are often filled with meat and cabbage or sauerkraut – another food supposedly brought west by the Mongols.

Also-rans: Bubble and Squeak, *Rotkohl* and Coleslaw

If cabbage and potatoes are the only vegetables you are eating anyway, why not put them together? The entirety of northern Europe seems to have spent centuries perfecting methods of combining cabbage and mashed potatoes: taking potatoes (mashed or not) and frying them with chopped cabbage as a hash (British bubble and squeak, Catalonian *trinxat*); mixing mashed potatoes with chopped cabbage and baking it (Scottish rumbledethumps); or boiling the cabbage and potatoes separately and then mashing them together (Irish colcannon, Dutch *stamppot* and Flemish *stoemp*). That said, early recipes for bubble and squeak consist of fried cabbage with beef, not potatoes. The first recorded 'recipe' is a spoof from a satire called *The Midwife, or Old Woman's Magazine* (1753). It calls for beef 'or any other meat' and cabbage 'that is most windy, and capable of producing the greatest report' – that is, farting – and to 'let it bubble and squeak over a charcoal fire for half an hour, three minutes, and two seconds.'

Maria Rundell's *A New System of Domestic Cookery* (1808 edn), published in England, calls for rare beef, while other authors call for 'boiled salt beef left from a dinner'. Francis Grose's *A Dictionary of the Vulgar Tongue* (1788 edn) defines bubble and squeak as 'Beef and cabbage fried together. It is so called from its bubbling up and squeaking whilst over the fire.' Other sources claim the 'squeak' is the sound of chopping and scraping a cast-iron frying pan with a metal scraper.

By 1888 potatoes were beginning to creep in, and a London slang dictionary called bubble and squeak 'a compound of meat fried up with potatoes and greens'. At some point – allegedly during the rationing of the Second World War, or perhaps the Great Depression – meat was cast aside altogether, and potatoes commenced their eternal reign.

The name 'coleslaw' was adapted from the Dutch *koolsla* near the end of the eighteenth century in the USA – yet another odd adaptation of Dutch to English-speakers' uses, like the geographic names Fresh Kills and Hell's Kitchen in New York. Initially called 'cold slaw' in 1794, by 1842 it had morphed into cole-slaw – a mixture of shredded cabbage and salad dressing or mayonnaise.

Germans, Czechs and Scandinavians serve sweet braised *Rotkohl* (red cabbage) in the autumn with their meats, making a spiced sweet-and-sour dish with apple, vinegar, red wine, cloves, juniper berries and a sweetener along the lines of sugar or redcurrant jam. Icelanders, whose pre-twentieth-century cuisine tended towards pickled herring and survival foods like brine-preserved sheep heads, adapted *rötekohl* from their Danish colonial masters. The sweet braised red cabbage is served with the Sunday roast of leg of lamb along with caramelized potatoes and brown sauce. Icelandic grandmothers who grew up after the Second World War remember when sugar was a luxury good, and reportedly douse their cabbage and potatoes with astonishing quantities of sugar.

These same northern European cabbage fans also came up with the grand idea of the *Grünkohlessen* (green kale eating) and *Kohlfahrt* (cabbage walk). These excuses for midwinter inebriation involve going to a local pub and eating a feast of kale, sausage and potatoes while drinking large quantities of alcohol. Participants who walk to a pub in the country are going on a *Kohlfahrt*, and drag a handcart with alcohol along the way for refreshment, but you can also take the bus to a *Grünkohlessen*.

In New Zealand, cabbage leaves are used to wrap meat and other foods for a traditional Maori *hangi*, a meal cooked by steaming a variety of foods over coals in a pit, similar to a New England clambake. Some resilient Kiwis cook an abbreviated *hangi* in slow-cookers, but still use cabbage to wrap their meats – which makes for a dull party but a convenient weeknight dinner.

Kimchi

Koreans use napa-cabbage-based kimchi in almost anything – to make meat-, fish-, tofu- or vegetable-based stews and soups, in omelettes or pancakes, with noodles or rice, or in sandwiches. Like garlic in the West, it is included in pretty much any apart from chocolate cake and ice cream.

It is difficult to come up with a single great ethnic cabbage dish for any of China's regions, simply because cabbage's culinary role is similar to that of pork, or water. It isn't used in every dish, but it is hard to avoid it, and it doesn't make any particular food special or particularly beloved.

Cabbage is also eaten elsewhere in the world – in Central and South America, in Africa, in South Asia – but it doesn't form the heart of any single cuisine outside of the northern latitudes. It is typically just one element in a stew, pilaf, soup or pastry. In El Salvador *curtido*, a type of salad-shredded cabbage pickled briefly in vinegar, is a common accompaniment to snacks called *pupusas* – pockets of cornmeal dough filled with meat or beans. But the *curtido* isn't strictly essential; it is not the sort of food young men dream about being served by their mothers when they are sleeping very far from home.

6
The Future of Cabbage

NASA has been investigating how to grow Chinese cabbage on the International Space Station. The canny NASA planners are smart. Cabbage consumption has been increasing steadily since 1961 . . . in China. Vegetable consumption in the developing world increased from 50 kg (110 lb) per person per year in 1961 to 118 kg (260 lb) per year in 2003, surpassing vegetable intake in developed countries. Most of that increase was in China, and most of the vegetables were brassicas – cabbages, mustards and their botanical pals.

Elsewhere on earth, cabbages are in trouble. Like many other troublesome, sulphurous foods, cabbage has been ignored by the fast-food industry, and increasingly by Western consumers.

In the U.S., since 1920 annual cabbage consumption per capita has declined from 10 kg (22 lb) to 3.7 kg (8.3 lb), and sauerkraut has slipped from 1 kg (2.2 lb) to 0.3 kg (0.7 lb) per person since 1970. The main reason it has not slipped away entirely is because red cabbage looks pretty in pre-cut salad mixes, and bags of coleslaw and stir-fry mixes are popular with harried home cooks. In the U.S., 45 per cent of all cabbage is processed into bland, forgettable coleslaw, 35 per cent sold as fresh cabbage, and 12 per cent is made into sauerkraut:

another 5–10 per cent is 'fresh cut products'. Cabbage's only notable resurgence in twentieth-century America was in the form of the Cabbage Patch Kids, a line of squash-faced dolls which were supposedly adopted out of vegetable farms and became enormously popular in the mid-1980s, provoking fisticuffs as desperate Christmas shoppers battled for the toys. In November 1984 the waiting list for Cabbage Patch Kids at just one New Jersey toy shop reached 10,000 names. Although the fad peaked in 1985, with $600 million in sales of all things Patchy, the Kids are still in production, and their manufacturer claims that more than 115 million dolls have emerged from their leafy wombs.

Germans are eating less sauerkraut, too – an ominous sign for a country where 85 per cent of cabbages are made into kraut. During the 1990s German sauerkraut consumption fell from 1.7 kg (3.7 lb) per person to 1.2 kg (2.6 lb) per person per year. Even Koreans are eschewing their kimchi. Average daily consumption of kimchi declined by roughly 20 per cent in South Korea from 1998 to 2012, from 50 kg (110 lb) per person annually to 41 kg (90 lb) – which is still a lot of kimchi.

The list goes on. In Poland during the last decade, researchers found that city-dwellers ate far less cabbage and far more tomatoes than country folk, and the effect is stronger the larger the size of the city. Portuguese consumption of all brassicas fell from 60 kg (132 lb) per person per year in the 1970s to less than a third of that by 2008, abandoning their *caldo verde* for paler foods (like french fries). In France, the sweet savoy cabbage grown in Lorient, Brittany, since the 1890s is disappearing. The Slow Food Foundation blames its decline on the arrival of kale, which is 'more pleasing to the eye and more standardized'.

Given the increasing urbanization of all countries, will cabbage eventually become extinct? Cabbages are also leery

Cabbage looper caterpillar, the subject of controversial biological pesticide research.

of our warming global climate. Temperatures above 30 °C (86 °F) reduce yields of cabbages not specifically bred for summer production, and seedlings of all varieties of cabbage – summer and winter – are killed at temperatures of 35 °C (91 °F) and above. These temperatures also wilt cabbages post-harvest. A scandal erupted in China in 2012, when enterprising cabbage-traders in Shandong were found to be employing a preservation technique more typically used on corpses in the West: formaldehyde. The carcinogenic embalming compound was being sprayed on cabbages to keep them from wilting, supposedly because the cabbage-growers could not afford refrigerated trucks. That was especially unfortunate because Shandong is famous for its napa cabbage, particularly the Jiaozhou city 'white cabbage'.

Cabbages are also a favourite food of pests. Modern geneticists are becoming ever more inventive in their quest to kill caterpillars, leading to controversy and endless Internet rumours. In 1994 a group of scientists in Oxfordshire sprayed a field of cabbage with a virus that infects cabbage looper caterpillars, who are not normally very popular creatures. This

Tokyo Bekana Chinese cabbage leaves prior to harvest aboard the International Space Station.

particular virus had been genetically modified to produce a toxin that is usually found in Algerian scorpions, giving rise to endless reports of 'scorpion venom cabbages' on the World Wide Web. This biopesticide does not seem to have gone into commercial production. An American team performing a similar contemporaneous experiment used a toxin produced by a tiny mite, and has generally escaped public censure.

Fewer people are eating cabbage, and it is getting harder to grow it. There is still hope, but that hope may not be on this earth. NASA has been testing LED lights on the International Space Station to grow greens – including lettuce, Swiss chard, radishes, peas and Chinese cabbage – on long space flights. Astronauts can learn from other extreme growing conditions; scientists at the South Pole station have been growing the cabbage's cousin bok choy for years.

Cabbage has already been featured in space flight at least twice. On 25 March 1961, the Soviet space programme launched a ship containing a mannequin nicknamed Ivan Ivanovich wearing the same models of spacesuit, ejection seat and parachute harness the human cosmonaut Yuri Gagarin would wear a month later. To test the radio system – and to reassure any Western eavesdroppers that there wasn't a secret spy mission going on – the ship's communications consisted of a tape loop repeating songs sung by a choir and instructions for making the Russian cabbage soup shchi, and borscht with beetroot.

When the first South Korean astronaut, Yi So-Yeon, journeyed to the International Space Station in 2008, she brought with her special space kimchi, a sterile condiment that took more than five years to develop. A kimchi full of the traditional fermenting bacteria would run the risk of infecting the space station with unanticipated organisms, or damaging equipment. 'Imagine if a bag of kimchi starts fermenting and bubbling out of control and bursts all over the sensitive equipment of the spaceship,' said Lee Ju Woon at the Korean Atomic Energy Research Institute, who used samples from his mother's kimchi to help develop the space-safe version. There were other concerns about eating kimchi in enclosed spaces as well. 'We managed to reduce the smell by one-third or by half so the other astronauts will feel comfortable trying our space kimchi,' said Kim Sung Soo, a Korea Food Research Institute scientist. Perhaps one day space-sauerkraut, fermented from a harvest from a garden aboard ship, will feed another voyager's soul as she journeys to sow cabbages among the stars.

Recipes

Soft Cabbage (*Olus molle*)
Apicius, *De re coquinaria* (The Art of Cooking), Book III,
The Gardener, *c.* 500 BCE

The cabbage is cooked with pot herbs in soda water; press the water out chop it very fine: now crush pepper, lovage, dry satury with dry onions, add stock, oil and wine.

[Satury is some type of dried herb: in Apicius's Book VII, he suggests oregano as an alternative.]

To make Salty Pickles of Mallow, Cabbage, Colza and Mustard Greens
Chi Min Yao Su, 'Important Arts for the Peoples' Welfare',
c. 533–544 CE, trans. Shi Sheng Sheng Han

Select leaves of good quality, and tie them in bunches with cattail [bulrush] stem. Prepare a solution of salt in water; make sure it is really salty. Wash the vegetables in the salty solution and place them in a jar. If they are first washed with fresh water the pickle will quickly deteriorate. After the salty wash water clarifies, pour enough of it into the jar to cover the vegetables. Do not move the vegetables around. At this point the colour of the vegetables is still green. If they are taken out, washed to remove the salt, and then cooked, they will taste as good as fresh vegetables.

Method for making blanched pickle: Chinese cabbage and turnip leaves are suitable for this treatment. Select good-quality vegetables. Blanch them in hot boiling water. If the vegetables have already started to wither, wash them with water, drain and allow them to recover their freshness overnight. Then blanch them. After blanching, plunge the vegetables briefly in cold water. Then mix them with salt and vinegar and season with cured sesame oil. The product will be fragrant and crisp. If a large batch is prepared, it can be kept until spring with no spoilage.

Cabbage Soup
Kitab al Tabij (c. 1150–1200), Moorish Spain, trans. Candida Martinelli
and Charles Perry

Take meat and cut up as fine as possible, and take old cheese, the best you can obtain, and cut it up, and throw on it an onion pounded with cilantro (coriander).

Take tender pieces of cabbage, and boil. And pound with all of this in a wooden mortar, and then throw in a pot. Boil once or twice.

Add some murri, a little vinegar and some pepper and caraway, and cover the contents of the pot with dough and brush with eggs.

How to Flavour Cabbage
Kitab Wasf Al-at'ima al-Mu'tada, 'The Description of Familiar Foods',
c. 1236, trans. Charles Perry (*A Baghdad Cookery Book*)

Take walnut meats and blanched almonds and toasted hazelnuts. Pound everything, then take caraway, which you toast and pound fine, and with it a little thyme and garlic seed. Then you perfume the cabbage with good oil. Then you take a little bit of vinegar; you dissolve the walnuts and ingredients with it. Then you throw on a sufficiency of tahiney, and let there be a little Syrian cheese with it. Add the spices to them and arrange them, then you throw the rest of the ingredients on the bowl. Then throw in some of the first spice, enough to perfume their taste and aroma. It is not eaten until the next day.

Caboches in Pottage
The Forme of Cury (1390)

Take Caboches and quarter hem and seeth hem in gode broth with Oynouns y mynced and the whyte of Lekes y slyt and corue smale and doer to safroun an salt and force it with powdour douce.

[Take cabbages and quarter them and boil them in good broth with minced onions and the white part of leeks slit and cut small. Add saffron and salt and sweet spices.]

Green Porray
Le Ménagier de Paris (1392), trans. Eileen Powers (1928)

Let it [a cabbage] have the outer leaves removed and be cut up and then washed in cold water without parboiling it and then cooked with verjuice and a little water, and put some salt therein, and let it be served boiling and very thick, not clear; and put at the bottom of the bowl, underneath the porray, salt butter, or fresh if you will, or cheese, or old verjuice.

Salted Vegetables
Gao Lian, *Zunsheng Bajian*
(Eight Treatises on the Nurturing of Life, 1591)

Remove cabbage root and yellowish leaves, wash cabbage clean and let it drain.

Sprinkle 10 jin of salt over 10 jin [5 kg] of cabbage leaves; put liquorice stems in a clean jar.

Sprinkle salt in between cabbage leaves and put them in the jar. Add a little bit of dill. Press down on it with hands and put several liquorice stems and a stone over it.

Three days later, turn leaves upside down; wring bittern out. Put the leaves again in clean jar. Pour bittern onto cabbage.

Seven days later, repeat the same process. Pour in clean water and put stone on top. This completes a tasty cabbage pickling.

One Pot Stew

Antonio de Solís, *Eurídice y Orfeo* (1643), trans. Carolyn Nadeau

> A one-pot stew, do you think it
> Appears miraculously?
> Shouldn't it have its mutton,
> Its fat back, its garbanzos,
> Its black pepper, its saffron,
> Its beef, its bits of garlic,
> Its parsley, its onion
> And its cabbage?

Cabbage Soup (*shchi*)

George Trevor, *Russia Ancient and Modern* (1862)

The cabbage-soup (*shtshee*) is the favourite national dish, and is variously prepared. Six or seven cabbages, chopped up, half a pound of barley-meal, a quarter of a pound of butter, a couple of pounds of mutton cut up, and a handful of salt, stewed in two cans of *kwass*, make an ordinary mess. The very poor omit the butter and mutton; the richer classes substitute broth for *kwass*, and enrich the dish with cream and other ingredients.

French Cabbage Soup

Adapted from Alexis Soyer, *The Modern Housewife; or, Ménagère* (1849)

> 4 l (1 gallon) water
> 1 kg (2 lb) salt pork or bacon
> 1 kg (2 lb) cabbage cut in strips

2 large onions, diced
1 carrot, diced
1 turnip, diced
2 stalks celery, chopped

Combine all ingredients and simmer for three to four hours until the pork is tender, skimming off fat. Season to taste with salt, black pepper or brown sugar. Pour over bread slices in a tureen and serve. In lieu of pork you may add 4 oz (¼ lb) of butter. Some make this dish using only cabbage.

Soyer comments, 'It is also frequently made *maigre* by omitting the pork or bacon adding more vegetables of all kinds and quarter of a pound of butter, and frequently where have nothing else but cabbage, they make it only of that; now, setting all national feeling aside respecting the poverty of their meals, I have known strong healthy men make a hearty meal of it, preferring it to meat, of which they scarcely ever partake.'

Garbure Gasconne

Adapted from *Jane Grigson's Vegetable Book* (1978),
The Country Cooking of France (2012) and *Classic Koffman* (2016)

15 g (½ oz) goose fat, duck fat or bacon grease for sautéing vegetables
2 onions, sliced
2 turnips, sliced
4 potatoes, diced
½ a medium green cabbage (*c.* 500 g (1 lb))
100 g (4 oz) salt pork
1 confit duck leg
optional: 150 g (5 oz) small white beans
for serving: thick slices of rustic bread

Melt the fat in a large stock pot. Add the vegetables and sauté until lightly browned. Add 3 litres (5 pints) of water and soaked beans, if using, simmer for a half-hour. Add the confit duck leg and simmer for another half-hour. Remove the solids from the broth and slice the pork and confit duck leg thinly. Layer the vegetables, meats and bread in a tureen. Pour the broth over the ingredients in the tureen and serve.

Cabbage-Jelly
The Family Economist, mid-nineteenth-century
English monthly magazine

A tasty little dish, and by some persons esteemed more wholesome than cabbage simply boiled. Boil cabbage in the usual way, and squeeze in a colander until perfectly dry. Then chop small; add a little butter, pepper and salt. Press the whole very closely into an earthenware mould, and bake one hour, either in a side oven or in front of the fire; when done, turn it out.

Bigos
Elena Molokhovets's recipe, 1861, from *Classic Russian Cooking: Elena Molokhovets' A Gift to Young Housewives*, trans. and introduced by Joyce Toomre (Bloomington, IN, 1998)

Hunter's stew from leftover beef with sauerkraut (*Bigos iz ostavshejsja zharenoj govjadiny, s kisloju kapustoju*). Line a saucepan with ¼ lb or more pork fat, add 3 glasses squeezed out, slightly soured cabbage [i.e. sauerkraut], and top with another ¼ lb pork fat or bacon. Pour on bouillon, cover with a lid, and stew. When the sauerkraut has half cooked, remove pork fat and cut it into small cubes together with the pork skin, Mix with the cooked beef, game, etc., cut up in the same manner. Stir the cubed meat and pork fat into the sauerkraut, sprinkle with pepper, and add ½ spoon flour fried until golden with 1 spoon butter and a finely chopped onion. Stew, covered, until the sauerkraut browns slightly, stirring often with a spoon to prevent the sauerkraut from burning. When the sauce boils away, everything may be turned out onto a platter. Pour butter fried with finely pounded rusks over the sauerkraut and mixed meats, bake, and serve for breakfast or for dinner before the bouillon.

A Ukrainian Grandmother's *Holubtsi* (Cabbage Rolls)
Adapted with permission from Mariia Yelizarova, 2016

Ingredients:
1 small cabbage (*c.* 900 g (2 lb))
250 g (½ lb) ground pork
250 g (½ lb) ground beef
300 g (1½ cups) cooked white rice
1 carrot, shredded
2 tbsp tomato purée
2–3 cloves of garlic, minced
2 tbsp sour cream
60 ml (¼ cup) water

Separate the cabbage into leaves. Fill a large stockpot or saucepan half-full with water, add a pinch of salt, and bring the water to a boil. Lower the leaves carefully into the boiling water and blanch them for two minutes. Remove cabbage leaves from the pot and drain.

Mix the ground pork and beef with the carrots, garlic, rice, and tomato purée.

To form the cabbage rolls, place two heaping tablespoons of the meat mixture in the centre of the cabbage leaf. Roll or wrap the leaf around the filling, then place the *holubtsi* seam-side down in a deep Dutch oven dish or cast-iron pot. When the pot is filled, pour ¼ cup of water over the rolls. Cover the top of the rolls with a mixture of sour cream and additional tomato purée if desired. Cook on very low heat for three hours or until fully cooked.

Sauerkraut

Adapted from Sandor Ellix Katz, *Wild Fermentation: The Flavor, Nutrition, and Craft of Live-culture Foods* (White River Junction, VT, 2003)

Timeframe: 1–4 weeks (or more)

Special Equipment:
Ceramic crock, food-grade plastic bucket, or 1-quart (*c.* 1-litre) glass or ceramic jar; do not use metals that may react with acid
Plate fits inside crock or bucket or water-filled plastic bag
Weight (a closed jar filled with water or clean rock), if using a plate
Cloth cover (a towel or cheesecloth)

Ingredients for 1 litre (1 quart):
500 g (1¼ lb) cabbage, chopped or grated
2½ teaspoon salt

Place grated cabbage in a large bowl. Sprinkle salt on cabbage and mix thoroughly. Pack cabbage mixture tightly into crock or jar, tamping it down with your hands, a wooden spoon, or a potato mixer to remove as much air as possible, and to force water out of the cabbage. Cover the cabbage mixture with either a plate and a weight, or a water-filled plastic bag that will cover the cabbage. The idea is to keep air from contacting the fermenting cabbage. Leave the cabbage mixture at room temperature

Wait 24 hours. The brine from the cabbage should have risen above the level of the cabbage mixture. If brine does not cover the mixture, add salt water to cover; mix 1 teaspoon salt with 250 ml water until dissolved and pour over the cabbage mixture until it is covered.

Leave the sauerkraut to ferment at a cool temperature, 18°C (65°F), for two days, then check. The sauerkraut will ferment faster at higher temperatures, slower at lower temperatures. When it reaches the level of sourness you prefer, remove the weight, close the jar, and move it to a refrigerator to slow fermentation. Enjoy as is, or in any recipe calling for sauerkraut.

Sauerkraut Cake

Adapted from The Old Foodie (TheOldFoodie.com)

There are many stories about how this recipe came about. Allegedly Mrs Geraldine Timms, supervisor of the lunchroom at Chicago's Waller High School in Chicago, created this memorable recipe in response to the United States Department of Agriculture's Surplus Committee's call to school lunchroom staff for recipes to use up an excess supply of sauerkraut. Other sources claim that it was an April Fool's joke recipe in Pennsylvania in the 1960s.

300 g (2¼ cups) sifted plain (all-purpose) flour
1 tsp baking powder
1 tsp baking soda
¼ teaspoon salt
70 g (½ cup) unsweetened cocoa
150 g (⅔ cup) butter
300 g (1½ cups) sugar
3 eggs
1 tsp vanilla
240 ml (1 cup) water
50 g (⅔ cup) rinsed, drained and chopped sauerkraut

Grease and flour two 20-cm (8-in.) round cake tins. On wax paper sift together the flour, baking powder, baking soda, salt and cocoa. In a large mixing bowl cream butter and sugar. Thoroughly beat in eggs, one at a time, and the vanilla. Stir in dry ingredients in four additions, alternately with water, until smooth each time; begin and end with dry ingredients. Stir in sauerkraut. Turn into prepared pans.

Bake in a preheated 180°C (350°F) oven until cake tester inserted in the centre comes out clean – thirty minutes. Place on wire rack to cool completely. Frost with your favourite frosting and serve.

Cabbage Confetti Quinoa

Adapted from Laura B. Russell, *Brassicas: Cooking with the World's Healthiest Vegetables: Kale, Cauliflower, Broccoli, Brussels Sprouts and More* (New York, 2012)

500 g (1 lb) red cabbage (½ a small head)
1 tablespoon butter or oil
2 large cloves of garlic, minced
1 tablespoon peeled, minced fresh ginger
1 red pepper, diced
½ teaspoon ground turmeric
¾ teaspoon kosher salt
250 ml (2 cups) cooked white quinoa

Heat butter, garlic and ginger in a large, deep frying pan over medium-high heat. When the mixture starts to sizzle, add the diced pepper and cook, stirring, until it begins to soften (about three minutes). Add cabbage, turmeric and ½ teaspoon salt and cook, stirring, until the cabbage wilts. Stir in quinoa and remaining salt. Cook until hot, about two minutes more. Serve hot or at room temperature.

Pork and Napa Cabbage Northern-style Chinese Dumplings

Adapted from Nina Simonds

400 g (4 cups) napa cabbage, minced
1 tsp salt
500 g (1 lb) lean ground pork butt
200 g (2 cups) finely minced Chinese garlic chives or 150 g
(1½ cups) chopped leeks and 1 tbsp minced garlic
2½ tbsp soy sauce
2 tbsp toasted sesame oil
1½ tbsp Chinese rice wine or sake
1½ tbsp minced ginger root
1½ tbsp cornflour (cornstarch)

50 dumpling skins (also called *gyoza* skins)
120 ml (½ cup) soy sauce
1 tbsp chopped garlic

Place the minced cabbage in a bowl, add salt and toss to mix. Let sit thirty minutes, then squeeze out as much water as possible.

Combine cabbage with ground pork, minced Chinese garlic chives or leek mixture, the 2½ tablespoons of soy sauce, sesame oil, rice wine, ginger root, and 1 tablespoon of the cornflour.

Dust a baking sheet or plate with cornflour. Place a teaspoon of the filling in the centre of a dumpling skin. Moisten the edge of the skin with water, then fold the skin to make a semicircle, and press the edges together. Arrange the finished dumplings on a plate dusted with cornflour.

Mix the soy sauce and chopped garlic to make a dipping sauce.

Heat 3 litres (3 quarts) of water in a large stock pot until boiling over high heat. Add half the dumplings, stir and return the water to a boil. Let the dumplings boil for five minutes, then remove them with a strainer or a slotted spoon. Bring the water back to a boil, add the remaining dumplings and cook. Serve immediately.

Kimchi Grapefruit Margarita
Adapted from Lauryn Chun, *The Kimchi Cookbook: 60 Traditional and Modern Ways to Make and Eat Kimchi* (Berkeley, CA, 2012)

240 ml (1 cup) tequila
½ fresh habanero pepper
240 ml (1 cup) napa cabbage kimchi
1 tablespoon kimchi juice
320 ml (1⅓) cups fresh pink grapefruit juice
4 slices pink grapefruit for garnish

Combine all ingredients except sliced grapefruit in a large bowl, and let sit for at least two hours to infuse. Strain to remove solids. Pour the strained mixture into four ice-filled glasses and garnish with grapefruit slices.

Select Bibliography

Albala, Ken, *Eating Right in the Renaissance* (Berkeley, CA, 2002)

Bloch-Dano, Evelyne, *Vegetables: A Biography* (Chicago, IL, 2012)

Davidson, Alan, ed., *The Oxford Companion to Food,* 3rd edn (Oxford, 2014)

Doyle, M. P., and R. L. Buchanan, eds, *Food Microbiology: Fundamentals and Frontiers*, 4th edn (Washington, DC, 2013)

Field, R. C., 'Cruciferous and Green Leafy Vegetables', in *The Cambridge World History of Food*, vol. i, ed. K. F. Kiple (Cambridge, 2000), pp. 288–97

Huang, H. T., 'Part v: Fermentations and Food Science', in *Science and Civilization in China*, vol. vi: *Biology and Biological Technology* (Cambridge, 2000), pp. 451–2

Kim, Kwangok, et al., *Kimchiology Series No. 1: Humanistic Understanding of Kimchi and Kimjang Culture* (Gwangchu City, 2014)

Macleod, A. J., and G. MacLeod, 'Effects of Variations in Cooking Times on Flavor Volatiles of Cabbage', *Journal of Food Science*, xxxv (1970), pp. 744–50

Maggioni, M., et al., 'Origin and Domestication of Cole Crops (*Brassica oleracea L.*): Linguistic and Literary Considerations', *Economic Botany*, LXIV (2010), pp. 109–23

Prakash, S., X. M. Wu and S. R. Bhat, 'History, Evolution, and Domestication of Brassica Crops', *Plant Breeding Reviews*, xxxv (2011)

Rupp, Rebecca, *How Carrots Won the Trojan War: Curious (but True) Stories of Common Vegetables* (North Adams, MA, 2011)

Saberi, Helen, *Cured, Smoked, and Fermented: Proceedings of the Oxford Symposium on Food and Cooking* (Oxford, 2011)

Theophrastus; Sir Arthur Hort, *Enquiry into Plants and Minor Works on Odours and Weather Signs, with an English Translation by Sir Arthur Hort*, vol. 1 (London, 1916)

Toomre, J., 'A Short History of Shchii', *Food in Motion: The Migration of Foodstuffs and Cookery Techniques: Proceedings: Oxford Symposium*, vol. 11, ed. Alan Davidson (Oxford, 1983)

Watts, D. C., *Dictionary of Plant Lore* (London, 2007)

Zeven, A. C., 'Sixteenth to Eighteenth Century Depictions of Cole Crops (*Brassica oleracea L.*), Turnips (*B. rapa L.*) and Radish (*Raphanus sativus L.*) from Flanders and the Present-day Netherlands', *Acta Hort*, 407 (1996), pp. 29–33

Cookbooks

Lauryn Chun with Olga Massov, *The Kimchi Cookbook: 60 Traditional and Modern Ways to Make and Eat Kimchi* (Berkeley, CA, 2012). This book includes clear, detailed instructions on the theory and practice of making a wide variety of classic and modern kimchis for all seasons, and recipes ranging from the classic Korean kimchi jigae stew to novelties including a kimchi grapefruit margarita cocktail.

Bridget Jones, *Recipes from a Polish Kitchen* (Secaucus, NJ, 1990). Although this book is not specifically devoted to cabbage per se, it features fourteen different recipes for classic Eastern European cabbage dishes, including stuffed cabbage leaves (*gołąbki*), sauerkraut soup (*kapusniak*) and *bigos* stew. Unfortunately, it is out of print. If it is unavailable, a similar cookbook of more recent vintage is Anne Applebaum and Danielle Crittenden, *From a Polish Country House Kitchen: 90 Recipes for the Ultimate Comfort Food* (San Francisco, CA, 2012).

Sandor Ellix Katz, *Wild Fermentation: The Flavor, Nutrition, and Craft of Live-culture Foods* (White River Junction, VT, 2003). This modern classic features detailed instructions on how to make sauerkraut, low-salt sauerkraut, and sauerkraut with wine, seaweed or caraway seeds.

Kim Man-Jo, Lee Kyou-Take, Lee O-Young, *The Kimchee Cookbook: Fiery Flavors and Cultural History of Korea's National Dish* (North Clarendon, VT, 1999). A beautifully illustrated book with intriguing information about the history of kimchi, though its kimchi recipes fail to mention the initial warm fermentation period (20°C/70°F) necessary before storing kimchi for long, cool-temperature fermenation. Readers already familiar with kimchi-making will find many intriguing traditional kimchi recipes; novices should stick to Chun's *The Kimchi Cookbook*.

Laura B. Russell, *Brassicas: Cooking with the World's Healthiest Vegetables: Kale, Cauliflower, Broccoli, Brussels Sprouts and More* (Berkeley, CA, 2012). This handsome book features contemporary recipes for an array of brassicas served with quinoa, avocados, fennel, red curry and other fashionable foods. You won't find classic recipes like cabbage rolls or bacon-cabbage soup here, but the author does include tips on techniques for cooking brassicas and reducing their odour.

Websites and Associations

European Union Brassica Growers' Association
www.loveyourgreens.co.uk

Healthy and Tasty Kimchi (The Korean Culture and
Information Service)
www.korea.net/NewsFocus/Culture/view?articleId=103591

Leafy Greens Council (U.S.)
www.leafy-greens.org

Multinational Brassica Genome Project
www.brassica.info

Sauerkraut Recipes
www.sauerkraut.com

World Institute of Kimchi
www.wikim.re.kr

Acknowledgements

I would like to thank Mariia Yelizarova, who generously shared her grandmother's prized *holubtsi* recipe; Gary Reineccius, University of Minnesota Department of Food Science and Nutrition, for answering my questions about folk remedies for cabbage odours; and my husband Scott for his unwavering support of my writing, and his tolerance for home cabbage fermentation experimentation.

Photo Acknowledgements

The author and publishers wish to express their thanks to the below sources of illustrative material and/or permission to reproduce it. Some locations of artworks are also given below, in the interests of brevity:

W. Atlee Burpee Company/Henry G. Gilbert Nursery and Seed Trade Catalog Collection, *Burpee's Farm Annual* (1882): p. 34; from Ibn Butlan, *Tacuinum sanitatis*: p. 19; from Lewis Carroll, *Through the Looking Glass and What Alice Found There* (London, 1897): p. 59; collection of the author: p. 55; from *The Farmers Magazine*, vol. v (1836): p. 54; Gemäldegalerie, Berlin: p. 83; from John Gerard, *The Herball, or, Generall historie of plantes, 1636* (London, 1597): pp. 25, 26; Hallwyl Museum: p. 20; Kendra Helmer/USAID: p. 85; Joseph Dalton Hooker, *Botany of the Antarctic Voyage* . . . (London, 1844): p. 28; iStock images/PeteKaras: p. 6; from Paul Kauffmann, *Fabrication de Choucroute* (Paris, 1902): p. 63; from Hermann Adolf Köhler, *Medizinal-Pflanzen in naturgetreuen Abbildungen und kurz erläuterndem Texte* (Berlin, 1887): p. 10 (top and bottom); Kunsthistorisches Museum: p. 35; from Herrad of Landsberg, *Hortus Deliciarium* (Strasberg, c. 1180): p. 52; Metropolitan Museum of Art: p. 84; Meg Muckenhoupt: pp. 15, 22, 24, 76, 94, 102; NASA: p. 112; from John Nunn, *Narrative of the Wreck of the 'Favourite' on the Island of Desolation: detailing the adventures, sufferings and privations of J. Nunn, a historical account of the Island, and its whale and seal fisheries* (London, 1850): p. 29; podstresje/Večer: p. 99; private collection: pp. 36, 45, 48, 79, 80;

Index

italic numbers refer to illustrations